Lecture Notes in Computer Science 13733

More information about this series at https://link.springer.com/bookseries/558

Shiping Chen · Rudrapatna K. Shyamasundar ·
Liang-Jie Zhang (Eds.)

Blockchain – ICBC 2022

5th International Conference
Held as part of the Services Conference Federation, SCF 2022
Honolulu, HI, USA, December 10–14, 2022
Proceedings

 Springer

Editors
Shiping Chen (iD)
CSIRO Data61 and UNSW
Canberra, ACT, Australia

Rudrapatna K. Shyamasundar
Indian Institute of Technology Bombay
Mumbai, India

Liang-Jie Zhang (iD)
Kingdee International Software Group Co.,
Ltd.
Shenzhen, China

ISSN 0302-9743   ISSN 1611-3349 (electronic)
Lecture Notes in Computer Science
ISBN 978-3-031-23494-1   ISBN 978-3-031-23495-8 (eBook)
https://doi.org/10.1007/978-3-031-23495-8

This Springer imprint is published by the registered company Springer Nature Switzerland AG
The registered company address is: Gewerbestrasse 11, 6330 Cham, Switzerland

Preface

The International Conference on Blockchain (ICBC) was an international forum for both researchers and industry practitioners to exchange the latest fundamental advances in the state-of-the-art technologies and best practices of blockchain, as well as emerging standards and research topics that will define the future of blockchain.

ICBC 2022 was one of the events of the Services Conference Federation event (SCF 2022), which had the following 10 collocated service-oriented sister conferences: the International Conference on Web Services (ICWS 2022), the International Conference on Cloud Computing (CLOUD 2022), the International Conference on Services Computing (SCC 2022), the International Conference on Big Data (BigData 2022), the International Conference on AI & Mobile Services (AIMS 2022), the International Conference on Metaverse (METAVERSE 2022), the International Conference on Internet of Things (ICIOT 2022), the International Conference on Cognitive Computing (ICCC 2022), the International Conference on Edge Computing (EDGE 2022), and the International Conference on Blockchain (ICBC 2022).

This volume presents the papers accepted at ICBC 2022. All topics regarding blockchain technologies, platforms, solutions, and business models aligned with the theme of ICBC. Topics of interest included new blockchain architectures, platform constructions, blockchain development, and blockchain services technologies, as well as standards and blockchain services innovation lifecycles, including enterprise modeling, business consulting, solution creation, services orchestration, services optimization, services management, services marketing, and business process integration and management.

We accepted 8 papers, including 7 full papers and 1 short paper. Each was reviewed and selected by at least three independent members of the Program Committee. We are pleased to thank the authors whose submissions and participation made this conference possible. We also want to express our thanks to the Program Committee members for their dedication in helping to organize the conference and review the submissions. We owe special thanks to the keynote speakers for their impressive talks.

December 2022

Shiping Chen
Rudrapatna K. Shyamasundar
Liang-Jie Zhang

Organization

Services Conference Federation (SCF 2022)

General Chairs

Ali Arsanjani	Google, USA
Wu Chou	Essenlix, USA

Program Chair

Liang-Jie Zhang	Kingdee International Software Group, China

CFO

Min Luo	Georgia Tech, USA

Operation Committee

Jing Zeng	China Gridcom, China
Yishuang Ning	Tsinghua University, China
Sheng He	Tsinghua University, China

Steering Committee

Calton Pu	Georgia Tech, USA
Liang-Jie Zhang	Kingdee International Software Group, China

ICBC 2022

Program Chairs

Shiping Chen	CSIRO Data61 & UNSW, Australia
Rudrapatna K. Shyamasundar	Indian Institute of Technology Bombay, India

Program Committee

Adel ElMessiry	ALPHAFIN, USA
Xinxin Fan	IoTeX, USA
Chao Li	Beijing Jiaotong University, China
Qinghua Lu	CSIRO, Australia
Qi Chai	IoTeX, USA

Rui Zhang   Institute of Information Engineering, Chinese
                                      Academy of Sciences, China
Catalin Meirosu   Ericsson, Sweden
Vallipuram Muthukkumarasamy   Griffith University, Australia
Alexander Semenov   University of Florida, USA
Andreas Veneris   University of Toronto, Canada
Lei Xu   Kent State University, USA
Zhiming Zhao   University of Amsterdam, The Netherlands
Arnab Chatterjee   R3, India

Services Society

The Services Society (S2) is a non-profit professional organization that was created to promote worldwide research and technical collaboration in services innovations among academia and industrial professionals. Its members are volunteers from industry and academia with common interests. S2 is registered in the USA as a "501(c) organization", which means that it is an American tax-exempt nonprofit organization. S2 collaborates with other professional organizations to sponsor or co-sponsor conferences and to promote an effective services curriculum in colleges and universities. S2 initiates and promotes a "Services University" program worldwide to bridge the gap between industrial needs and university instruction.

The Services Society has formed Special Interest Groups (SIGs) to support technology- and domain-specific professional activities:

- Special Interest Group on Web Services (SIG-WS)
- Special Interest Group on Services Computing (SIG-SC)
- Special Interest Group on Services Industry (SIG-SI)
- Special Interest Group on Big Data (SIG-BD)
- Special Interest Group on Cloud Computing (SIG-CLOUD)
- Special Interest Group on Artificial Intelligence (SIG-AI)
- Special Interest Group on Edge Computing (SIG-EC)
- Special Interest Group on Cognitive Computing (SIG-CC)
- Special Interest Group on Blockchain (SIG-BC)
- Special Interest Group on Internet of Things (SIG-IOT)
- Special Interest Group on Metaverse (SIG-Metaverse)

Services Conference Federation (SCF)

As the founding member of SCF, the first International Conference on Web Services (ICWS) was held in June 2003 in Las Vegas, USA. The First International Conference on Web Services - Europe 2003 (ICWS-Europe'03) was held in Germany in October 2003. ICWS-Europe'03 was an extended event of the 2003 International Conference on Web Services (ICWS 2003) in Europe. In 2004 ICWS-Europe changed to the European Conference on Web Services (ECOWS), which was held in Erfurt, Germany.

SCF 2019 was held successfully during June 25–30, 2019 in San Diego, USA. Affected by COVID-19, SCF 2020 was held online successfully during September 18–20, 2020, and SCF 2021 was held virtually during December 10–14, 2021.

Celebrating its 20-year birthday, the 2022 Services Conference Federation (SCF 2022, www.icws.org) was a hybrid conference with a physical onsite in Honolulu, Hawaii, USA, satellite sessions in Shenzhen, Guangdong, China, and also online sessions for those who could not attend onsite. All virtual conference presentations were given via prerecorded videos in December 10–14, 2022 through the BigMarker Video Broadcasting Platform: https://www.bigmarker.com/series/services-conference-federati/series_summit

Just like SCF 2022, SCF 2023 will most likely be a hybrid conference with physical onsite and virtual sessions online, it will be held in September 2023.

To present a new format and to improve the impact of the conference, we are also planning an Automatic Webinar which will be presented by experts in various fields. All the invited talks will be given via prerecorded videos and will be broadcast in a live-like format recursively by two session channels during the conference period. Each invited talk will be converted into an on-demand webinar right after the conference.

In the past 19 years, the ICWS community has expanded from Web engineering innovations to scientific research for the whole services industry. Service delivery platforms have been expanded to mobile platforms, the Internet of Things, cloud computing, and edge computing. The services ecosystem has been enabled gradually, with value added and intelligence embedded through enabling technologies such as Big Data, artificial intelligence, and cognitive computing. In the coming years, all transactions involving multiple parties will be transformed to blockchain.

Based on technology trends and best practices in the field, the Services Conference Federation (SCF) will continue to serve as a forum for all services-related conferences. SCF 2022 defined the future of the new ABCDE (AI, Blockchain, Cloud, Big Data & IOT). We are very proud to announce that SCF 2023's 10 colocated theme topic conferences will all center around "services", while each will focus on exploring different themes (Web-based services, cloud-based services, Big Data-based services, services innovation lifecycles, AI-driven ubiquitous services, blockchain-driven trust service ecosystems, Metaverse services and applications, and emerging service-oriented technologies).

The 10 colocated SCF 2023 conferences will be sponsored by the Services Society, the world-leading not-for-profit organization dedicated to serving more than 30,000 services computing researchers and practitioners worldwide. A bigger platform means bigger opportunities for all volunteers, authors, and participants. Meanwhile, Springer will provide sponsorship for Best Paper Awards. All 10 conference proceedings of SCF 2023 will be published by Springer, and to date the SCF proceedings have been indexed in the ISI Conference Proceedings Citation Index (included in the Web of Science), the Engineering Index EI (Compendex and Inspec databases), DBLP, Google Scholar, IO-Port, MathSciNet, Scopus, and ZbMath.

SCF 2023 will continue to leverage the invented Conference Blockchain Model (CBM) to innovate the organizing practices for all 10 conferences. Senior researchers in the field are welcome to submit proposals to serve as CBM ambassadors for individual conferences.

SCF 2023 Events

The 2023 edition of the Services Conference Federation (SCF) will include 10 service-oriented conferences: ICWS, CLOUD, SCC, BigData Congress, AIMS, METAVERSE, ICIOT, EDGE, ICCC and ICBC.

The 2023 International Conference on Web Services (ICWS 2023, http://icws.org/2023) will be the flagship theme-topic conference for Web-centric services, enabling technologies and applications.

The 2023 International Conference on Cloud Computing (CLOUD 2023, http://thecloudcomputing.org/2023) will be the flagship theme-topic conference for resource sharing, utility-like usage models, IaaS, PaaS, and SaaS.

The 2023 International Conference on Big Data (BigData 2023, http://bigdatacongress.org/2023) will be the theme-topic conference for data sourcing, data processing, data analysis, data-driven decision-making, and data-centric applications.

The 2023 International Conference on Services Computing (SCC 2023, http://thescc.org/2023) will be the flagship theme-topic conference for leveraging the latest computing technologies to design, develop, deploy, operate, manage, modernize, and redesign business services.

The 2023 International Conference on AI & Mobile Services (AIMS 2023, http://ai1000.org/2023) will be a theme-topic conference for artificial intelligence, neural networks, machine learning, training data sets, AI scenarios, AI delivery channels, and AI supporting infrastructures, as well as mobile Internet services. AIMS will bring AI to mobile devices and other channels.

The 2023 International Conference on Metaverse (Metaverse 2023, http://www.metaverse1000.org/2023) will focus on innovations of the services industry, including financial services, education services, transportation services, energy services, government services, manufacturing services, consulting services, and other industry services.

The 2023 International Conference on Cognitive Computing (ICCC 2023, http://thecognitivecomputing.org/2023) will focus on leveraging the latest computing technologies to simulate, model, implement, and realize cognitive sensing and brain operating systems.

The 2023 International Conference on Internet of Things (ICIOT 2023, http://iciot.org/2023) will focus on the science, technology, and applications of IOT device innovations as well as IOT services in various solution scenarios.

The 2023 International Conference on Edge Computing (EDGE 2023, http://the edgecomputing.org/2023) will be a theme-topic conference for leveraging the latest computing technologies to enable localized device connections, edge gateways, edge applications, edge-cloud interactions, edge-user experiences, and edge business models.

The 2023 International Conference on Blockchain (ICBC 2023, http://blockc hain1000.org/2023) will concentrate on all aspects of blockchain, including digital currencies, distributed application development, industry-specific blockchains, public blockchains, community blockchains, private blockchains, blockchain-based services, and enabling technologies.

Contents

Research Track

Insights on Impact of Distributed Ledgers on Provider Networks

David Guzman[1,2]($\boxtimes$) (iD), Dirk Trossen[1], Mike McBride[3] (iD), and Xinxin Fan[4] (iD)

[1] Huawei Technologies, Munich, Germany
{david.guzman,dirk.trossen}@huawei.com
[2] Technical University of Munich, Munich, Germany
[3] Futurewei Technologies, Santa Clara, CA 95050, USA
michael.mcbride@futurewei.com
[4] IoTeX, Menlo Park, CA 94025, USA
xinxin@iotex.io

Abstract. Internet scale distributed consensus takes advantage of randomized algorithms to cope with functional resilience, reliability and access while accomplishing decentralized agreement at expenses of costly unicast communication. This paper provides experimental insights on randomized communication patterns for distributed consensus systems. We define, measure and approximate communication overhead against key performance indicators like latency and communication overhead, leading to a discussion on how network innovations may mitigate the identified issues. While this paper does not promote specific solutions or DLT implementations, our initial insights invite the wider community working on DLT and network solutions alike to deepen those insights to aid future research and development into solutions, concepts, and technologies.

Keywords: Distributed consensus · Permissionless · Networking

1 Introduction

Large scale distributed systems execute functionality, often called *smart contract*, while keeping track of transactional information in distributed databases. It is crucial that the information in those databases represents a consensus among its participants to ensure its veracity. For this, so-called 'permissioned systems' may be utilized where the distribution across authenticated and trusted parties is realized through well-known, e.g., publish-subscribe communication patterns. The trust assumption, however, poses a strong requirement on deploying such systems, often limiting their scalability. For this reason, 'permissionless systems' aim at removing this strong assumption, effectively allowing anybody to join the distributed consensus process, thereby decentralizing the operations across anybody who is willing to commit resources to do so. Blockchains [1], as an example for Distributed Ledger Technologies (DLT) [2], represent a category of solutions for such permissionless systems.

The removal of the strong trust assumption, however, comes with its own challenges. In order to ensure functional resilience and reliability against any

S. Chen et al. (Eds.): ICBC 2022, LNCS 13733, pp. 3–17, 2022.
https://doi.org/10.1007/978-3-031-23495-8_1

random peer in the system to disappear or stop functioning, randomized algorithms are employed so as to not only utilize highly randomized members of the overall pool of resources but also to spread information across random peers to remove any reliance on any single peer due to the lacking trust into its operations and trustworthiness.

These randomized algorithms find realization in (i) a discovery algorithm that is in charge of assuring a sufficiently large sample of peers from the entire network to be contacted, (ii) a *diffusion multipoint* communication based upon the discovered peer topology, pursuing a so-called atomic broadcast [3] to commit and forward blocks and transactions. Given the randomized nature of both of those key processes, there is a clear impact on the system's key performance indicators (KPIs), such as completion time for a transaction but also costs for those transactions and managing the topology.

Motivated by our preliminary work in [4] we structure, analyze, and discuss the performance and costs of such randomized communication algorithms and their impact on provider networks. Measurement and analysis of the P2P statistical nature have been carried out for Ethereum in [5,6]. However, we lack studies that analyze peer reachability, privacy, and information propagation while implementing a randomized discovery phase as well as the costs for signaling and the resulting communication establishment latency and efficiency for a diffusion multipoint operation.

Consequently, we summarize our contributions as: (i) striving for a *structured understanding* on communication patterns, and (ii) assessing the *impact and costs* of communication patterns based on KPIs, real measurements, and statistical approximations. While our work focuses on the Ethereum P2P network for its insights, we are confident that our results can be easily validated, replicated, and scaled to other implementations of large scale decentralized consensus systems.

For this, we first analyze the core interactions and communication patterns between Ethereum peers in the peer discovery, establishment process, and consensus requirements in Sect. 2. Based on the observed P2P communication patterns, we then identify in Sect. 3 a number of challenges with respect to peer reachability and their required capabilities, the realization of transaction communication across the DLT, as well as privacy and/or security threats. Through our extensive experiments, we quantify in Sect. 4 the inefficiencies of the Ethereum P2P network along key performance indicators such as latency communication overhead, and effective data consumption. We further confirm and compare the approximate statistical distributions of our topological measurements with results in [5,6]. In Sect. 5, we use these observations and insights to discuss a number of research and innovation opportunities for improving on the observed situation, before concluding the paper in Sect. 6.

2 Communication in a DLT

There has been ample work, such as [1,3,4], including in standardization organizations, such as the IEEE [7,8] and the IRTF/IETF [9], on defining main DLT concepts. We focus our brief introduction on those concepts most important from a communication perspective. We first outline the interactions at a higher level before delving into the communication patterns that result from those.

2.1 DLT Interactions

We can distinguish three core interactions in a DLT:

A client commits a **transaction** to the DLT, which is diffused across a set of DLT miners, which in turn respond separately, adding the transaction to their internal ledger information. Committing the transaction leads to the miners assigning compute and storage resources to the smart contract that underlies the transaction. For this, so-called *proofs* are executed, although some methods for proof require additional communication to take place, e.g., election protocols.

The result of the proof is a **block** (of ledger information), committed to a set of DLT miners, which each receiving miner adds to their internal blockchain.

A client may query the latest **blockchain** from a set of miners to which the query is sent. The longest returned blockchain represents the most trustworthy ledger information.

In the following subsection, we focus on the communication patterns that are utilized to achieve the aforementioned interactions. Special attention is given on the establishment of the needed peer-to-peer network, used in the randomized multipoint operations that are executed for each interaction, be it a transaction or the commitment of a newfound block.

2.2 Resulting Communication Patterns

Key for exchanging information in the DLT P2P network is to establish and maintain a *pool of DLT peers*, representing a subset of the larger set of all DLT peers. We differentiate two types of peer relations, namely those actively initiated by a peer and those maintained as a result of a received request to initiate a relation due to other peers also actively seeking relations. We call the former *outgoing peer* and the latter *incoming peer* in the following.

The details on how this pool is established and maintained are obtained from Ethereum [10], containing platform-specific aspects, which likely differ from those used in other platform; however, the main concepts remain the same.

Figure 1 outlines the necessary steps, divided into a) *discovery* of outgoing DLT peers, and b) *establishment* of the pool of DLT peers, ultimately used to for the randomized interaction patterns outlined in the previous sub-section.

More specifically, the discovery phase in Fig. 1a aims at building a *list of outgoing DLT peers* through actively seeking relationships with other peers. For this, the DLT peer first seeds the selection through information obtained from pre-configured so-called *bootstrap peers*. This set of neighbours is randomized (Step

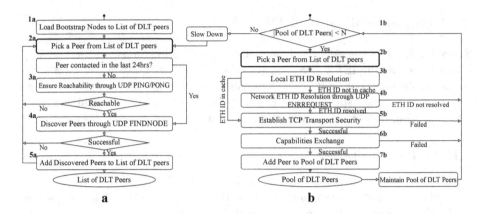

Fig. 1. (a) Discovery of outgoing peers, (b) Establishing pool of peers

2a) and tested for *reachability* through a UDP-based PING/PONG exchange with a default timeout of 500 ms. Any non-reachable peer, i.e., those timing out, are removed from the list of outgoing peers.

All remaining nodes are now tested for *neighbourhood information*, sending a UDP-based FINDNODE request, which is responded positively as a NEIGHBORS response that includes a list of (usually 16, as defined by configuration) DLT peers, in the form of their IP addresses and supporting ports, while removing any timed-out DLT peer from the list.

Through repeating the neighbour peer discovery with the above steps in intervals of 500 ms, the list of outgoing DLT peers grows. Upon reaching a configured length N (set to a default of 50 in a standard Ethereum configuration), the peer discovery is slowed down with discovery intervals growing up to 30 min. The final size of the list of outgoing DLT peers is a matter of local limitations, with Sect. 4.3 outlining typical list sizes obtained from our experiments.

The list of outgoing DLT peers, as candidates for relationships, is now extended into a *pool of DLT peers* as active TCP connections to a subset of DLT peers. Figure 1b) shows the necessary steps for the creation of that pool.

Key difference to the list of outgoing DLT peers in step 2a is that the pool of DLT peers includes those actively created during the discovery phase as well as any incoming peers, i.e., connections initiated by other peers that are undergoing the same process of DLT pool establishment. The limit for the desired DLT pool size is equal to N, i.e., the same number for the initial limit for the list of outgoing peers. However, the pool establishment limits the number of outgoing peers to one third of this pool size, while the rest is reserved for incoming peers. Hence, a candidate for adding to the pool of DLT peers can either be selected from the list of outgoing peers (as long the configured limit has not been reached) or through accepting an incoming peer connection.

For both cases, the Ethereum ID, uniquely identifying the DLT peer in the Ethereum P2P network, is being resolved next, either through obtaining a locally cached value (for any DLT peer that has been previously resolved) in step 3b or through sending a UDP-based ENRREQUEST request to the chosen DLT peer in step 4b. Next, transport layer security is established, utilizing TLS-based mechanisms [10,11]. If successful, a capability exchange takes place, determining bilateral support for, e.g., hash functions, needed hardware capabilities (such as GPUs) or others, to successfully complete any requests. If capabilities match, the DLT peer (and its connection information) is added to the pool of DLT peers. For all operations, a default timeout of 35 s is configured that when reached, sees the contacted DLT peer being discarded (i.e., removed from the pool of DLT peers) and the process returning to the initial step.

The steps of adding a single peer to the pool is repeated until the target size N is reached. At this point, the pool is maintained rather than further extended. For this, any failing DLT peer connection is being removed from the pool and another peer is being added, either actively as an outgoing DLT peer or by waiting for another incoming establishment request, depending on the type of the failed peer and committed to the proportion of incoming and outgoing peers. Furthermore, any incoming DLT establishment request is being responded to, leading to removing an existing incoming DLT peer from the pool if the connection to the new incoming DLT peer is ultimately successful. Outgoing peers are replenished after a time interval, depending on the type of transaction, after which the DLT peer is being replaced with another from the list of outgoing DLT peers. Through these methods, the DLT pool is constantly replenished with randomly renewed DLT peers albeit with a continuing cost for doing so.

Transactions, realizing the interaction patterns outlined in Sect. 2.1 utilize the pool of DLT peers by sending their requests to all peers in the pool. This sending of transactions may even start already while the pool creation is still ongoing, i.e., once a suitable peer can be obtained from the overall (and still growing) pool of DLT peers. However, transactions will not finish until the requests will have been sent to the number of DLT peers defined as the pool size, i.e., N. With this, latencies for initial transactions are directly dependent on the time it takes to fully establish the pool.

3   Challenges for Users and Provider Networks

Considering the observed communication patterns, we can identify a number of challenges that need better understanding; our results in Sect. 4 will quantify some of the aspects related to those challenges.

1. **Costs for pool maintenance:** Reachability information is required to interact with other peers. As illustrated in Fig. 1, new DLT peers need to continuously establish and maintain suitable reachability information, resulting in each DLT peer maintaining a constantly changing pool of DLT peers as active (TCP) connections.
2. **Costs for resilience and reliability:** During the pool establishment and maintenance, peers may never reply to connection attempts, resulting in additional latency due to timeouts, prolonging the establishment of the pool of

peers to communicate with. Furthermore, peers added to the pool may fail throughout their lifetime, leading to (timeout-inducing) removal from the pool, requiring to replenish the pool with another suitable peer.

3. **Need to match capabilities:** Peers do not know about other peers' capabilities to serve requests when contacting them or being contacted by them. While the discovery in Fig. 1a ensures possible reachability, only the pool establishment (Fig. 1b) guarantees successful communication with a matching peer, while a capability mismatch leads to discarding the peer and attempting a connection with a new peer albeit having already created costs for the connection to the mismatching peer.

4. **Unicast replication:** We can see from the interactions in Sect. 2.1 that communication in a DLT is *multipoint* in nature, i.e., transactions or information (such as blocks) are sent to the entire pool of DLT peers, not just a single one. Given the mechanisms explained in Sect. 2.2, this pool of DLT peers is a randomized subset of the larger overall DLT overlay with the intention to achieve *diffusion* among many DLT peers. This avoids repeated communication with a fixed set of DLT peers, reducing the threat of collusion of information through a malicious set of DLT peer, and ultimately ensure consensus. The consequence of that varying random nature of the multipoint diffusion, however, is that repeated unicast replication (at the initiating DLT peer) is used instead of efficient network-level multicast, which negatively impacts efficiency and transaction completion time.

5. **IP address privacy:** DLT peers need to expose their IP address to the DLT system, replicated to the bootstrap nodes and DLT peers by virtue of the discovery process outlined in Fig. 1. This leads to privacy and/or security issues, enabling geo-identification of peers, DoS attacks on particular parts of the DLT, and others.

4   Experimental Insights

Our insights to quantify aspects on the aforementioned challenges were obtained through an Ethereum based experiment, using the *go-ethereum release V1.10-stable* on a Linux-based machine, operating out of Munich, Germany. For our experiments, we used the same setup as described in [4], with more details and initial insights to be found in [4].

We constructed the experiment to complete a first transaction that any new peer will initiate as a requirement to be part of the DLT network, namely to download the latest agreed blockchain from the DLT network. For this, the peer initiates a so-called *full synchronization* to replicate the latest full blockchain from the DLT network, where full (and light) synchronization are configurations for a peer to obtain replicas of the blockchain. The latest blockchain is identified by a *checkpoint*, which is agreed and disseminated in the DLT system.

For this, the initiating peer realizes the steps in Fig. 1 to build the pool of DLT peers, over which to execute requests such as *commit* transactions, *diffuse* blocks, as well as to execute a full synchronization. The necessary discovery and communication establishment steps are performed over a geographic spread which included all continents albeit with an expected clustering of nodes across North America, Europe, Asia, and Australia, with only few discovered in South America and Africa as shown in Fig. 2a.

As outlined before, we categorize communication relations for an initiating peer into outgoing (OUT) and incoming (IN). Furthermore, we define a synchronization process as a *local warm start* when caches for the outgoing relations are re-used from a previous execution, as opposed to a *local cold start*, which empties any caches before starting. Note that a local cold start does not assure a remote cold start, leading to the possibility of stale information in the remote cache compared to any newly discovered information in the local cache; we did not specifically explore the impact of this issue, e.g., on security of the P2P network.

In our setup, we configure our peer according to a default configuration, thereby seeking to establish relations with $N = 50$ peers, out of which $O = 17$ are outgoing, and $I = 33$ are incoming relations. With each run, we execute an unsynchronized *geth* client in warm-start with the goal to ultimately download a full blockchain. Hence, each run re-uses the caches from previous runs, and we set an interval of 2 [min] between each new run, all executed during the months of January to June of 2022.

4.1 Topological Measurements

Let us first outline our insights on the topological relations created through the pool establishment and maintenance operations outlined in Fig. 1.

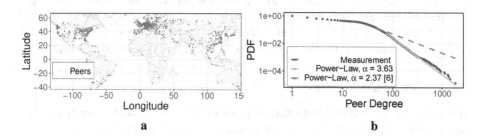

Fig. 2. (a) Peer geographic distribution, (b) Peer degree distribution

Through our experiment, we discovered 71.5k *active* peers, spread globally as depicted in Fig. 2a. This scale is comparable to the one reported in [5, Section IV-A], 74k in experiments taking place between December 2018 and January 2019, where 30 parity nodes were used only for peer discovery.

In Fig. 2a, we identify two main clusters of around 200 peers in North America and in Europe, while clear tails on the geographic distribution can be visualized for Asia, South America, Africa and Australia ranging from clusters of 10−20 peers. This geographic topology impacts and shapes the statistical properties of the distributed system KPIs, as we discuss in the following sections.

We measure the random variable (RV) *peer degree* over the discovered topology, depicting its distribution in Fig. 2b together with its heavy-tail approximation and compared to the one in [6, Section 4]. This distribution is characterized by a small-degree (≤71) phase and a tail (≤1844), confirming a plausible Power Law (PL) distribution as already reported in [5, Section 4.C], and [6, Section 4]. In order to formalize these observations, we apply [12] with the conclusion that a PL distribution approximation fits our empirical data tail. Thus, we assert that our measurements are representative, while capturing key communication patterns, and can therefore be replicated, validated and scaled.

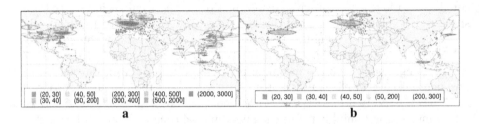

Fig. 3. (a) Incoming connection reachability, (b) Outgoing connection reachability

In Fig. 3, the *long tails* are exposed as a measure of reachability, manifesting the same clustering behaviour as in the geographic topology. Here, we can notice that incoming communication relations in Fig. 3a are ≈ 10× greater than outgoing communication relations in Fig. 3b. We believe that is caused through possible geo-policies that determine to reach certain peers in specific locations. For instance, peers in Asia are clearly less likely to establish successfully an outgoing communication relation than peers in North America and Europe.

4.2 Types of DLT Peers

One insight is the differentiation into *types of DLT peers* that stem from the communication patterns in Fig. 1, specifically the following types:

Non reachable peers include all peers that do not positively respond to Step 3a of the discovery or step 4b in pool establishment. Reasons here are that those peers may be located behind a firewall, be intermittently available (and switched off during the connection attempt), or simply have left the DLT while still remaining in the list of DLT peers maintained at other peers.

Signalling peers include those that respond positively to reachability but do not positively succeed in the various signalling steps for the DLT pool inclusion, i.e. step 4a in the discovery phase or the various steps during the pool establishment phase (ETH-ID resolution in Step 4b, TCP handshake and secure context establishment in Step 5b, or capability exchange in Step 6b).

Potential data peers successfully complete all steps in Fig. 1, adding them to the pool of peers for transfer of DLT-relevant data. Through the mechanisms in Fig. 1, potential data peers are constantly replenished, leading to the high ratio of potential data peers to actual data and dropped data peers.

Data peers are the subset of potential data peers that successfully transfer DLT-relevant data.

Dropped data peers are the subset of potential data peers that do not successfully transfer DLT-relevant data. The reasons here are unavailable or outdated information, or not completing the transfer since blockchain information may be several GB large. Hence, while communication does take place, it is not successful with respect to the intended communication.

Table 1. Type of peers

Peer	Outgoing [%]	Avg.	Incoming [%]	Avg.
Non-reachable	5.17	353.22	0.01	1.87
Signaling	87.1	6011.29	76.78	10259.56
Potential data	7.73	540.7	23.19	3098.35
Data	0.002	0.111	0.013	1.667
Dropped data	0.005	0.302	0.005	0.302

Table 1 shows that around 93% and 77% of all attempted relations fail either due to lack of reachability or mismatching capabilities for outgoing and incoming relations respectively. We focus on the costs associated with those failures.

4.3   Costs for Pool Establishment and Maintenance

For outlining the potential costs for the communication patterns in Fig. 1, we focussed on the following key performance indicators (KPIs) of random nature for our insights to follow:

1. *Pool Establishment Time* for the initiating peer to build the configured ($N = 50$) pool size.
2. *Pool Establishment Cost* as the relation of the number of peers which established successful communication compared to the total amount of attempted peers until the time of reaching full pool size.
3. *Effective Data Consumption* as the amount of useful data being retrieved from the DLT (i.e. a valid blockchain) versus the total downloaded data.

Pool Establishment Time. Figure 4a shows an example iteration that runs until the pool of DLT peers is completed. Here, we identify two main phases when establishing such pool. First, the interval $0 < t \leq t_{N/3}$, where attempts for outgoing connections (O_{trials}) are executed until the number of outgoing connections reaches a third of the total amount of connections. Second, the

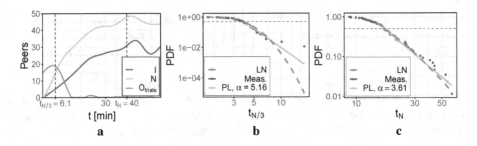

Fig. 4. (a) Single sample for pool establishment time, (b) $t_{N/3}$, (c) t_N

interval $t_{N/3} < t \leq t_N$, where the main contributors to the pool N are inbound connections I. After the initiating peer established its outgoing connections, these are maintained during this second period as needed. For instance, we can see the initiation of another outgoing connection at $t = 25\,\mathrm{min}$, likely due to an existing connection failing at that time. In the sample, the first interval is reached after 6.1[min], and the second one at 40[min].

The RVs $t_{N/3}$ and t_N are measured and approximated for the entire experiment in Fig. 4b and Fig. 4c, respectively [12]. Over the total amount of iterations, the outgoing establishment limit, $t_{N/3}$, is reached at 4min with 50% probability, while the time to complete a pool of DLT peers is reached at 20 min with 50% probability, as depicted in Figs. 4a and 4b, respectively. It is worth noting that for both RVs a PL and a Log-Normal(LN) approximation are a plausible fit for our measurements.

Pool Establishment Cost. For this KPI, we divide costs into those for peer discovery and for pool establishment:

Peer Discovery. For the sample in Fig. 4a, a total of 1.9k peers were contacted (Fig. 1-Step 2a, UDP PING) out of which reachability with 1.6k peers was ensured (Fig. 1-Step 2a, UDP PONG), while 151 peers replied to the discovery (Fig. 1-Step 4a, UDP NEIGHBORS). Overall, about 5k peers were added to the list, significantly less than the size of active DLT peers [13].

Table 2. Discovery cost summary

RV	Outgoing						Incoming					
	Power-Law			Log-Normal			Power-Law			Log-Normal		
	α	x_{min}	p	μ	σ^2	x_{min}	α	x_{min}	p	μ	σ^2	x_{min}
Attempts	5.24	604	0.2	6.31	0.38	336	4.6	620	0.58	6.47	0.37	423
Reachability	3.87	346	**0.03**	6.04	0.41	257	4.58	619	0.59	6.47	0.37	423
Disc. attempt	6.22	269	0.79	5.61	0.21	164	3.59	732	0.16	6.79	0.41	480
Disc. success	6.16	161	**0.04**	5.07	0.21	98	3.86	785	0.11	6.72	0.43	459

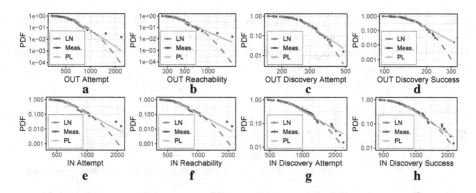

Fig. 5. (a–d) Outgoing, and (e–h) incoming discovery KPI distributions

As before, we analyze the short and long term distribution behaviour for the RVs that are part of the pool establishment cost in the peer discovery phase. In Fig. 5, we show a compilation of the outgoing and incoming communication relation distributions. Here, we notice that only the outgoing reachability and discovery success RVs are non-plausible PL distributions in its tails, due to its p-value in Table 2, which in turn is due to its truncated protocol execution that is bounded by the communication relations rate $\frac{out}{in} = \frac{1}{3}$.

Aligned with the results in Fig. 5 and parameters in Table 2, we procede to compare these RVs for outgoing communication relations in Fig. 6a, and for incoming communication relations in Fig. 6b. First, for outgoing communication relations with probability 50%: $\approx$ 77% of the contacted peers are reachable, out of these peers $\approx$ 63% are used to further topology discovery, and $\approx$ 57% successfully executed a complete discovery protocol. Second, for incoming communication relations almost all the reachability requests were positively replied by our peer, and $\approx$ 94% of the discovery requests are successfully completed. Finally, for the long tail, based on the PL approximation we estimate that for outgoing relations with probability 25%: $\approx$ 77.5% of peers were reached, with $\approx$ 33.9% selected for requesting a discovery and $\approx$ 31.46% successfully completing such discovery. Here, we can observe that only about one third (36%) of reachable peers are used to perform an actual successful discovery request. The last is due to reachability tests are *severely oversubscribed* through stacked pending PING requests, leading to additional communication waste.

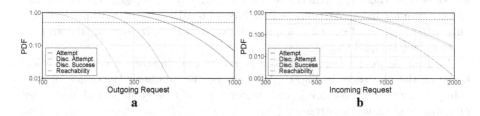

Fig. 6. (a) Outgoing, and (b) Incoming discovery cost

Pool Establishment. For the sample in Fig. 4a, 6.7k peers establish incoming communication to our peer, out of which 1.5k peers were successfully added to the pool. Further, outgoing attempts to 1.8k peers were created, out of which 153 peers were added to the pool.

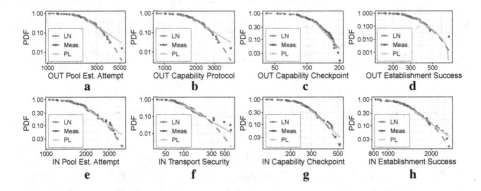

Fig. 7. (a–d) Outgoing, and (e–h) incoming pool establishment KPI distributions

Table 3. Pool establishment cost summary

RV	Outgoing						Incoming					
	Power-Law			Log-Normal			Power-Law			Log-Normal		
	α	x_{min}	p	μ	σ^2	x_{min}	α	x_{min}	p	μ	σ^2	x_{min}
Attempts	4.52	2250	0.33	7.78	0.29	1041	4.81	1973	0.43	7.6	0.29	1063
Transport security	3.6	23	0.69	3.09	0.56	5	3.03	93	0.62	4.63	0.62	36
Capability protocol	4.37	1777	0.25	7.57	0.3	845	6.71	83	0.86	4.32	0.26	44
Capability checkpoint	5.31	114	0.25	4.73	0.31	42	5.52	286	0.46	5.63	0.28	127
Establishment success	6.21	350	0.26	5.74	0.28	144	5.04	1383	0.75	7.24	0.3	825

For the whole experiment, the estimated minimum number of incoming peers was 1k peers, out of which 0.8k peers were added to the pool, i.e., a 77.6% success rate for a LN approximation. For outgoing peers, 1.04k peers were attempted, out of which 144 peers were added to the pool, i.e., a success rate of only 13.83% as exposed in Table 3. Furthermore, for the long tail phase, Figs. 7e and 7h, the success rate for incoming peers is 70% based on a PL approximation. And, for outgoing peers based on a PL approximation and Figs. 7a and 7d, the success performance is equal to 15%.

In Table 3, we further divide the attempts and failures of communication based on the sequences in Fig. 1b. We first list the number of incoming or outgoing attempts, i.e., how many peers undergo the discovery steps and how many outgoing and incoming attempts trigger the establishment steps in Fig. 1. The second row shows the amount of peers which failed either resolving an ETHID, establishing a three-way-handshake TCP or negotiating RLPx security [14]. Further, we mark peers not meeting a capability requirement, e.g., the ETH protocol, while row 4 shows peers at which the checkpointed blockchain was not available. Ultimately, the last row shows the number of peer that were included into the pool of DLT peers.

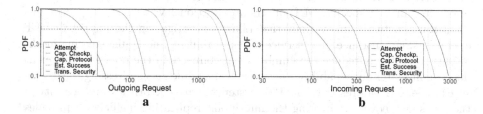

Fig. 8. (a) Outgoing, and (b) Incoming pool establishment cost

Noteworthy in our above results are the discrepancies between failures of incoming and outgoing connections in Fig. 8. For instance, outgoing peers have significantly higher transport and security failures, where 82% of errors occur while trying to decrypt the remote secret and find the proper blockchain checkpoint, and 18% I/O errors (invalid ciphertext length, unexpected end of file); we currently explain this issue with stored but outdated cypher information, while outgoing connections (of a new peer) start afresh in their cypher information.

Effective Data Consumption. The total downloaded data amounted to 3168G, out of which 892G were data added to the local blockchain, while 2276G were dropped. We interpret this as an effective data consumption ratio of 28.15%.

5   Discussion

Let us take our insights to outline an agenda for future investigations.

Increasing insights: The results and insights in this paper, e.g., in respect to communication patterns and incurred costs for networks, are only the start. As a more immediate steps, quantifying the costs outlined in the previous section in respect to the total number of bytes sent over the network would provide a more direct cost relation to the transport network. Furthermore, as outlined in Sect. 2.2, the multipoint replication incurs significant costs on the network; specifying those transmission costs would provide a basis for any potential improved network mechanism addressing this aspect of DLTs. Also, insights on topology dependence, e.g., for localized DLTs in comparison to wide-area DLTs, would be another route for investigation.

Extension to other DLT types: This paper is limited to a Proof of Work (PoW) based system, Ethereum, which in turn defines the communication patterns to realize the interactions within such system. Extending our insights into other DLT types, such as those utilizing different ledger validation techniques, is key. Our ultimate goal here is to develop a methodology that allows for studying DLTs more generally, e.g., in the form the P2P topology is maintained, the way communication is randomized and others, and compare DLTs in terms of the costs they incur when realizing those general aspects.

Network innovations: While the results in this paper may lead to improvements in realizing specific DLTs at the application level, we see opportunities for possible network innovations that allow for mitigating the impact of DLT operations. For instance, new service-oriented routing and traffic steering mechanisms [15,16] may reduce the number of disconnects in the pool establishment due to non-matching capabilities between peers, while also addressing the disclosure of peers' IP addresses to the P2P system to improve privacy and security of the peers. Moreover, addressing the multipoint replication inefficiency provides a significant, albeit challenging opportunity for network innovations.

Relation to ongoing standardization efforts: Standardization organizations, such as the IETF or the IEEE through side meetings and dedicated contributions, have been investigating various aspects of DLTs as a technology enabler for decentralized network and application functions. We believe, however, that our insights provide useful input into those standardization efforts in providing experimental evidence, albeit so far underspecified impacts that DLTs may bring, guiding the development of future DLTs and their supporting network functions to ensure efficient communication in real-life deployments.

6 Conclusion

The increasing use of DLT at Internet scale has led us to question the possible impact on provider networks. When looking closer at the interactions in a typical DLT, we have identified that inefficiency and waste are important factors that may negatively impact further adoption of DLTs. Understanding the reasons behind both is paramount for thinking of alternatives, both for the use of DLTs (if that is possible within the remit of the considered application) and the realization over provider networks through novel network solutions. With our statistically analyzed empirical insights, this paper serves as a starting point for a wider dialogue on the use and impact of DLTs and its core randomized algorithms, the relation with and use within provider networks, and the opportunities for addressing the identified problems through new innovation and standardization activities alike.

References

1. Dotan, M., Pignolet, Y.-A., Schmid, S., Tochner, S., Zohar, A.: Survey on blockchain networking: context, state-of-the-art, challenges. ACM Comput. Surv. **54**(5), 1–34 (2021). https://doi.org/10.1145/3453161

2. Bellaj, B., Ouaddah, A., Bertin, E., Crespi, N., Mezrioui, A.: SOK: a comprehensive survey on distributed ledger technologies. In: IEEE International Conference on Blockchain and Cryptocurrency (ICBC), vol. 2022, pp. 1–16 (2022)
3. Howard, H.: Technical report, no. 935 (2019)
4. Trossen, D., Guzman, D., McBride, M., Fan, X.: Impact of distributed ledgers on provider networks, no. 935 (2021)
5. Gao, Y., Shi, J., Wang, X., Tan, Q., Zhao, C., Yin, Z.: Topology measurement and analysis on ethereum p2p network. In: 2019 IEEE Symposium on Computers and Communications (ISCC), pp. 1–7 (2019)
6. Wang, T., Zhao, C., Yang, Q., Zhang, S., Liew, S.C.: "Ethna : analyzing the underlying peer-to-peer network of ethereum blockchain, pp. 1–15 (2021)
7. IEEE, P2958: standard for a decentralized identity and access management framework for internet of things. Technical report (2020)
8. IEEE, P3210: standard for blockchain-based digital identity system framework. Technical report (2020)
9. IETF, Decentralized internet infrastructure (dinrg). Technical report (2022)
10. Ethereum, Go ethereum official client (2022). https://github.com/ethereum/
11. Rescorla, E.: The transport layer security (TLS) protocol version 1.3, IETF, RFC 8446 (2018). http://tools.ietf.org/rfc/rfc8446.txt
12. Clauset, A., Shalizi, C.R., Newman, M.E.: Power-law distributions in empirical data. SIAM Rev. 51(4), 661–703 (2009). https://doi.org/10.1137/070710111
13. Ethereum, "Etherscan," (2022). https://etherscan.io/nodetracker
14. Ethereum, "Ethereum developers," (2022). https://ethereum.org/en/developers/docs/
15. Glebke, R., Trossen, D., Kunze, I., Lou, Z., Rüth, J., Stoffers, M., Wehrle, K.: Service-based forwarding via programmable dataplanes. In: 1st International Workshop on Semantic Addressing and Routing for Future Networks (2021)
16. Khandaker, K., Trossen, D., Khalili, R., Despotovic, Z., Hecker, A., Carle, J.: Cards: dealing a new hand in reducing service request completion times. In: IFIP Networking (2022)

Legal Service Delivery and Support for the DAO Ecosystem

Larry Bridgesmith[1], Adel ELMessiry[2](✉), and Mohamed Marei[3]

[1] Vanderbilt Law School, ASU Sandra Day O'Connor College of Law, Phoenix, USA
[2] WebDBTech, Bucharest, USA
`Adel.ElMessiry@gmail.com`
[3] Ministry of Justice, Cairo, Egypt

Abstract. The Distributed Autonomous Organization (DAO) development community seeks to decentralize decision making and reduce the imposition of non-consensual constraints on organizational operations to the greatest extent possible. Deploying blockchain, cryptocurrency, smart contracts and Artificial Intelligence applications, a virtual organization can be created through emerging technologies which functions autonomously in a decentralized manner. A DAO allows its members to democratize decision making through approved rules and policies which are executed automatically consistent with the group's decentralized decisions. In contrast, the world's legal systems and the enforcement of their decisions represent a highly centralized approach to making agreements and resolving disputes that arise from them. This paper will make the case for and recommend the operational details of a new and complete legal ecosystem for the DAO community. Deploying the benefits of decentralized decision making and problem solving, LegalDAOs can be developed to augment distributed autonomous consensus serving the community in lieu of coercive, hierarchical and non-consensual decision making.

Keywords: DAO · Blockchain governance · Legal systems

1 Introduction

The impact of centralized systems of governance, products and services might be best illustrated by a recent account of an initiative by Mark Cuban, the billionaire entrepreneur, philanthropist and owner of the NBA Dallas Maverick's professional basketball team. Cuban was approached by a friend and pharmacist who introduced him to the highly profitable US system of retail prescription drug sales. Cuban cites the instance of a lifesaving drug to combat leukemia, which is sold under a perversely centralized supply chain model that insures the drug manufacturer will receive over $9000US for a prescription which he sells to consumers for $47US at Cost Plus Drugs, the company he founded.

Of course, this example can be duplicated countless times by reference to legal services [1], consumer products [2], currency exchange [3] and even the

S. Chen et al. (Eds.): ICBC 2022, LNCS 13733, pp. 18–28, 2022.
https://doi.org/10.1007/978-3-031-23495-8_2

administration of justice [4]. Whenever a product or a service depends on multiple players to deliver a desired commodity, a supply chain is required. Supply chain management has become an essential discipline deployed to reduce the waste and delay occasioned when multiple providers are neither integrated nor even concerned about the cost to the consumer of getting the product or service to the purchaser.

Centralized control of the supply chain was the only tool available for managing waste and insuring quality. However, with the growth of Blockchain (distributed ledger technology) [5], decentralized control became a means of improving the quality and speed of supply chains while eliminating waste and reducing economic costs [6]. Treiblmaier, makes the case that only Blockchain applications can satisfactorily address and improve the "triple bottom lines" of the supply chain's goals for social, economic and environmental sustainability as shown in Fig. 1.

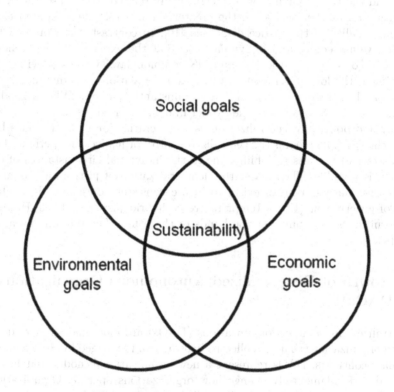

Fig. 1. Triple bottom line goal system.

The presenting question is, "Under whose control will these complex and multidisciplinary decisions be made?" Blockchain applications may be distributed, but they can also be controlled in a centralized manner (and most are). The terms and conditions of the use of a Blockchain application are generally determined by a small group of owners as applicable to all users in a take it or leave it manner [7]. The "consensus protocol" is the core approval filter through which each blockchain validates and executes transactions. The foundation of decentralized blockchain functionality is technologically driven by a centralized functionality determined by a few [8]. This article proposes a functional decentralization of blockchain technology can be more fully achieved through Decentralized Autonomous Organizations (DAOs), DAO's operating in legally enforceable and protected fashion are the tools by which the theory of democratized and decentralized operations of blockchain can be realized.

2   Current State of Centralized Legal Systems

Legal systems which attempt to eliminate disparities of outcomes (injustice) are highly centralized dispensers of legal rights and remedies [9]. The French Revolution and the rise of Civil Law are intrinsically related (code based law). The less discretion at the local level, the greater the control a legal system exerts over the equality of the justice dispensed [10]. In contrast, the Common Law tradition values equity and individual justice at the expense of consistency of outcomes. For example, the UK and US common law systems provide great discretion at the local level (courts, legislation, regulation) to individualize outcomes based on regional, societal and circumstantial factors. What's good for the goose isn't always good for the gander in democratized justice systems. Historically and politically, centralization vs. democratization of justice have been binary choices. The greater the centralized control of justice (civil, criminal and administrative) the less variability due to the individual circumstances of each situation is possible. The greater the democratization of justice individual circumstances, the less control exists to insure consistent outcomes. Republican forms of government (US) attempt to create hybrid justice systems. However, each form of justice suffers at the hands of the other. The tension is real and persists.

3   Growth of Decentralized Autonomous Organizations (DAOs)

Decentralized autonomous organizations (DAOs) are blockchain-native, decentralized organizations that are collectively owned and managed by their members via smart contracts. DAOs represent a new organizational model that has the potential to fundamentally change how organizations operate. Organizational innovations associated with the rise of DAOs are enabled by a novel technological infrastructure. Blockchain technology serves as the platform on which DAOs are set up. Blockchain technology refers to a distributed and digital ledger that records transactions in a transparent and immutable way. The advent of blockchain technology had a major impact on the business world and is one of the major pillars of the movement towards a decentralized economy [11] and a decentralized financial system, partly driven by new ventures' tokenizations through initial coin offerings (ICOs) [12]. The authors further distinguish DAOs from traditional top-down organizational structures such as corporations: DAOs operate through public and distributed decision-making, in which any DAO member can typically put forward proposals for any type of corporate decision and vote on them. This framework facilitates collaboration and community engagement among all members of the DAO that share common goals and ideals. Not all commentators view DAOs in such idyllic terms. Some criticize the reality of DAO's as mere exploitation by the haves of the have nots. Comparing DAO theory to cybernetics ("The Californian Ideology"), one author argues: Some scholars warn against these unchecked visions of decentralized, autonomous futures arguing that the ideological promises of the uses of decentralized technologies, such as widening political participation, contradict the reality of these tools in practice which inevitably collapse into re-centralisation under the forces of commerce as a powerful driver of technological innovation [13]. Regardless, the relative recency of the advent of DAO's holds promise that forms of self- governance may yet evolve to improve upon the state sponsored versions of democracy with their many unfulfilled promises. An early exploration of the origin of DAOs attributes Bitcoin founder(s) as the creator of the first DAO [14]. Bitcoin's blockchain application replicates the function of decentralized decision makers by virtue of the miners who manage the value and exchange of cryptocurrency. In contrast, the centralized features of banks maintain all transactional records on a single ledger requiring customers to trust the bank's accounting as accurate. Since Bitcoin's emergence, thousands of DAOs have been created with widely divergent purposes. DAOs have been created as:

- Investment DAOs in which individuals, friends, and colleagues form clubs to invest in web3 startups;
- Collector DAOs which acquire NFTs;
- Social DAOs that convene web3 communities;
- Collective/Cooperative DAOs in which groups of artists and engineers deliver services to other DAOs;
- Charitable DAOs that promote good causes and public interest;
- DAOs to own real property;
- DAOs to cap carbon emissions:
- DAOs to perform drone deliveries;
- DAOs to provide banking or other financial services;
- DAOs to run a business;
- DAOs which partner with other existing businesses;
- DAOs to launch satellites, and;
- DAOs to promote any number of real-world purposes [15].

In other words, if an association/organization of humans exist for any agreed upon goal for profit or non-profit purposes, a DAO can be created to support those needs [16]. Thus, the tensions between democratic and republican forms of government persist in the self-governing technology functionalities of blockchain.

4 Need for New Legal Applications for the DAO Development Community

In terms of the passage of time, traditional wisdom holds that legal rules and policies follow technology developments by a significant order of magnitude. However, other analysis depicts a more strategic approach adopted by platform technologies to delay governmental involvement in order to build influence and data mass [17]. It is not coincidental that Facebook's theme has been "move fast and break things" and Uber's has been "it's better to beg forgiveness than ask permission" [17]. Whether intention or neglect, legal developments rarely maintain pace with emerging technologies. It is for this reason DAO's currently have amazing opportunities to generate self-governance models which might positively influence the inevitable legal oversight to follow. DAO evangelists are fond of promoting the independence of their organizations as unbound by legal constraints due to the democratized self-governing nature of this new business structure. In their most canonical incarnations, DAOs operate without any formal legal recognition, eschewing dependence on governmental authority for their existence, and resisting the rigidity imposed on them by regulations. The result: pseudonymous, distributed, and ad hoc organizationalstructures [18]. This purist view from the perspective of technological possibilities fails to consider an essential need of all organizations: the ability to deal with and enter into enforceable agreements with other entities than the DAO itself. The legal rights, responsibilities, and remedies of associations of individuals are only ignored at their peril. Should the members of a DAO wish to contract with a bank or service provider vendor or enter into a joint enterprise, what are the applicable legal rights applicable to each? Despite the code efficacy of a smart contract, can all legal eventualities be anticipated? Clearly not. Therefore, what rights does the DAO have to enforce its expectations and resolve disputes with its members and other entities if not correctly captured in the autonomously executed terms of a smart contract? For example, the options for legally recognized organizational models were not prepared for the unique nature of DAOs. Because there was no square hole in which to force this round peg, legal analysts opined that DAO's must be like legal partnerships [18]. However, there are many additional organizational structures which could apply to DAO's, including:

- US Models
  - Unincorporated DAOs
  - Corporation
  - Limited Liability Company
  - DAO LLC
  - Nonprofit
  - Private Foundations and Public Charities
  - Political Nonprofit
  - Social Clubs
  - Unincorporated Nonprofit Association
  - Limited Cooperative Associations

  – International Models
    • Ownerless Foundations
    • Guernsey Special Purpose Trust [18]

Between the many purposes and the many structural forms, DAO founders would be ill advised to make a decision about the "legal wrapper" that best suits its purposes without experienced legal counsel's input and/or assistance. The choices and their consequences have led two states in the US (at the time of this writing) to create a unique statutory form of organization for DAO's. These legislative enactments address some of the deficiencies of the current list of options. Specifically, the inferred partnership model that courts might be inclined to adopt would impose "joint and several liability" on all the members of the DAO. This is a Draconian result that would allow a successful legal claim (from a member, customer, vendor, lawyer or other entity) to be owed equally by all the members. This outcome would permit a successful claimant to collect the value of the recovery from any one or all of the members up to the total sum of the claim. Wyoming [19] and Tennessee [20] enacted remedial statutes in 2021 and 2022 to address this concern. Both statutes require DAO formation documents, charters, articles of incorporation, operational agreements and name to clearly reflect the uniqueness of the DAO's nature. They each provide limited liability protections similar to those afforded LLC's under their state's laws. Whether DAO's can create a completely self-governed set of enforceable policies and procedures akin to these statutes and continue to operate outside a jurisdictional governance model remains to be seen. The concept of enforcement implies resort to a dispute resolution system which is jurisdictionally binding on the entity, its members and others who might pursue legal claims. Unless every agreement made by the DAO with others can reduced to an automated smart contract with payment provisions in the event of breach, and dispute resolution mechanisms which automatically operate, this outcome seems impractical and unlikely. Therefore, much remains to be done by the DAO community to achieve these additional legal protections. The following are suggested DAO organizations created to explore these potentials.

4.1 Legal System Reform DAO

The DAO ecosystem is comprised of many different legal, professional and economic interests. The entities and individuals that could be impacted by the growth of DAO development include at least the following:

  – Founders
  – Voting Members
  – Non-voting Associates
  – Engineers
  – Developers
  – Vendors
  – Customers
  – Legal Advisors

- Legal Jurisdictions (federal, state and local)
  - Taxing authorities
  - Investment regulators
  - Policymakers
  - Courts
  - Enforcement authorities
- Shareholders
- Media outlets
- Academic Institutions
- Standard Setting Bodies (ISO, IEEE, etc.)
- Etc., etc., etc.

A more diverse and potentially conflicted set of interests cannot be imagined. This writer's experience in implementing new technology with a large stakeholder group was ultimately successful after a botched initial effort [21]. A subsequent project proceeded far more effectively and efficiently because of the deliberate attention paid and the engagement of the many stakeholders impacted by the technology [22]. This process does not require active approval involvement by all stakeholders. However, obtaining input, adjusting the project plan and keeping stakeholders informed is critical to success bringing technology to fruition by users, owners and those impacted by it. DAOs are an organizational tool by which these obstacles can be addressed. A DAO created to categorize, analyze and recommend legal reforms could govern the impact of DAO development in the most inclusive and democratized manner. A legal reform DAO could be established to provide voting membership to the key decisionmakers and informational/input to those impacted. Legal reform DAOs could be created for local, state, and national legal reform initiatives to involve and inform policymakers on the key attributes of DAO regulation and enforcement. DAOs can provide a pre-regulation platform by which issues can be addressed and interests protected to provide recommended language and content for adoption by legislative bodies. Facilitated legislative creation is most likely to achieve adoption and implementation. Brummer and Seira categorize similar organizations as Lobby DAOs. However DAOs which engage more stakeholders than just the advocates for a position could have more influence through the processes of facilitated decision making.

4.2 Dispute Resolution DAOs

A major concern for the growth of the DAO ecosystem pertains to the mechanisms by which disputes are addressed arising from the functions of the DAO and the smart contracts which govern agreements reached by the DAO [23]. Although the self-governing nature of DAO's and the automated functions of smart contracts will lessen the occurrence of disputes, it is unreasonable to suggest all disputes will be eliminated exclusively through technology [24]. In view of the economic value of assets maintained and managed by many DAOs, unresolved disputes could be hugely consequential. Even if the DAO's self-governance models maintain robust dispute resolution mechanisms for members and associates, the same cannot be said for those outside the DAO with whom the organization reaches agreements for services and products. Reliance on traditional models of dispute resolution may not fully meet the needs of the DAO community and those with whom it may work. The very thought of bringing the types of disputes which involve the technologies of smart contracts, decentralized organizations, blockchain, NFTs and cryptocurrency to a state court judge and/or jury is soul shatteringly frightening. The traditional dispute resolution options of courts, state sponsored specialty tribunals, self-regulating industry schemes, mediation, arbitration, and online dispute resolution processes all leave much to be desired when confronted with the complexity of DAO formation, operation and functionality. The knowledge and wisdom needed to meaningfully address the types of disputes DAOs encounter requires extraordinary expertise and experience possessed by an extraordinarily small group of processes and people. Sims further reports on the growth of Decentralized Dispute Resolution Services (DDRS) platforms for DAOs. As with all great ideas, improvements over time lead to far better solutions than originally envisioned. As a result, DDRSs are coming online with sophisticated and variable options for disputants depending on the nature of the dispute. To date there are no autonomous dispute resolution systems available. They all involve some level of human engagement or judgment. Functioning like DAOs, some DDRSs provide voting and staking privileges for decision makers. Typically decentralized and blockchain based, the primary distinctives between the current processes available relates to the degree to which outcomes are determined by reference to the law of jurisdictional systems and enforceable in state sponsored adjudication entities (i.e. courts). Many DDRSs eschew government involvement. As these DDRS systems continue to mature, utilization and incorporation of their services will undoubtedly become more central to the smart contracts which govern DAOs and others doing business with them.

4.3 Legal Wrappers and Legal Support DAO for DAOs

The tension between total technological democratization and any degree of centralized decision making inherent in the DAO ecosystem also applies to the application of law and legal systems to their functionality. Purists would have their DAO exist independently of state oversight or involvement and rely on completely autonomous self-governing mechanisms. That day may come, but has yet to arrive. Like the promise of General Artificial Intelligence, until machines can replicate in all ways the capacities of the human brain, we will have to rely on Narrow Artificial Intelligence as the primary advanced technology tool to process data and recommend decisions. Humans are still needed to exercise judgment. In the meantime, the practicalities of organizational rights, responsibilities and liabilities to others remains a reality to be managed for the benefit of the DAO's purposes. As a natural result, ignoring the impact of legal systems will only complicate and expose the DAO to greater risk and responsibility than the organizers, founders, members and associates ever envisioned. Therefore, strategic thought and counsel need to go into choosing a legal framework within which the DAO will best thrive and be least encumbered. In terms of organizational identity, many forms of legal entities exist. In the US currently, the states of Wyoming and Tennessee have enacted enabling legislation to protect DAO's from the unintended consequences of joint and several liability imposed by inference on general partnerships. Additionally, Delaware has recognized the legitimacy of any "records administered to be stored on one or more distributed electronic networks or databases" In addition, in 2018 Malta created a framework for decentralized entities governed by AI [25]. However, it has no applicability to DAO's governed by people. The legislation in Wyoming and Tennessee are the best current examples of legal wrappers for DAOs to date that recognize and protect much of their unique nature while limiting liabilities. In addition, DAOs could be formed to feature global resources available to organizers and founders of these unique forms of organizational entities to provide the best legal counsel for their specific needs. Using a reputational DAO format [26] these listed legal resources (lawyers, law firms, alternative legal service providers and consultants) could create a trusted marketplace for the availability of legal advice and counsel on the myriad of issues confronting DAOs.

5   Conclusion

Since their origin, DAOs have demonstrated potentially transformational impact on the interests of the economy, law, organizational governance and individual rights. Much remains to be developed in order to increase the acceptance and implementation of DAOs in order to realize the potential for positive change they can bring. This paper merely seeks to summarize how they have come to be and highlight the potential challenges and opportunities DAOs must confront to improve the legal frameworks within which they can optimally function. This writer commits to be on the journey along with the development of DAOs to help improve their chances of success as law strives to catch up with technology.

Acknowledgment. The authors would like to acknowledge AlphaFin, DEVxDAO, and Casper Labs for their support.

References

1. The Legal Supply ChainThis is the fifteenth in a series of articles about how corporate, R.G.S., government law departments can improve their performance, add measurable value to the organizations. It has been 27 years since the DuP, M.t.L.S.C.: Managing the legal supply chain (2020). https://www.legalbusinessworld.com/post/2020/01/20/managing-the-legal-supply-chain
2. Alicke, K., Rexhausen, D., Seyfert, A.: Supply chain 4.0 in consumer goods (2019). https://www.mckinsey.com/industries/consumer-packaged-goods/our-insights/supply-chain-4-0-in-consumer-goods
3. Geismar, H.N., Sriskandarajah, C., Zhu, Y.: A review of operational issues in managing physical currency supply chains. Prod. Oper. Manage. **26**(6), 976–996 (2016). https://doi.org/10.1111/poms.12593

4. Seepma, A.P., Donk, D.P., Blok, C.: On publicness theory and its implications for supply chain integration: the case of criminal justice supply chains. J. Supply Chain Manage. **57**(3), 72–103 (2020). https://doi.org/10.1111/jscm.12245

5. ElMessiry, M., ElMessiry, A.: Blockchain framework for textile supply chain management. In: Chen, S., Wang, H., Zhang, L.-J. (eds.) ICBC 2018. LNCS, vol. 10974, pp. 213–227. Springer, Cham (2018). https://doi.org/10.1007/978-3-319-94478-4_15

6. Treiblmaier, H.: Combining blockchain technology and the physical internet to achieve triple bottom line sustainability: a comprehensive research agenda for modern logistics and supply chain management. Logistics **3**(1), 10 (2019). https://doi.org/10.3390/logistics3010010

7. Elmessiry, A., Bridgesmith, L.: A call for an artificial intelligence constitution. Available at SSRN 4120592 (2022)

8. Cho, H.: Asic-resistance of multi-hash proof-of-work mechanisms for blockchain consensus protocols. IEEE Access **6**, 66210–66222 (2018). https://doi.org/10.1109/access.2018.2878895

9. Crettez, B., Deffains, B., Musy, O.: Legal centralization: a Tocquevillian view. J. Legal Stud. **47**(2), 295–323 (2018). https://doi.org/10.1086/698860

10. Johnston-Walsh, L., Steenhuis, Q., Colarusso, D., Bridgesmith, L., Elmessiry, A.: COVID & the practice of law: impacts of legal technology symposium issue. Akron Law Rev. **54**(4) (2020)

11. ElMessiry, M., ElMessiry, A., ElMessiry, M.: Dual token blockchain economy framework. In: Joshi, J., Nepal, S., Zhang, Q., Zhang, L.-J. (eds.) ICBC 2019. LNCS, vol. 11521, pp. 157–170. Springer, Cham (2019). https://doi.org/10.1007/978-3-030-23404-1_11

12. Bellavitis, C., Fisch, C., Momtaz, P.P.: The rise of decentralized autonomous organizations (DAOs): a first empirical glimpse. SSRN Electron. J. (2022). https://doi.org/10.2139/ssrn.4074833

13. Nabben, K.: Imagining human-machine futures: blockchain-based decentralized autonomous organizations. SSRN Electron. J. (2021). https://doi.org/10.2139/ssrn.3953623

14. Hsieh, Y.-Y., Vergne, J.-P.: Bitcoin and the rise of decentralized autonomous organizations. J. Organ. Des. **7**(1), 1–16 (2018). https://doi.org/10.1186/s41469-018-0038-1

15. Jennings, M., Kerr, D.: A legal framework for decentralized autonomous organizations - a16z crypto. https://a16zcrypto.com/wp-content/uploads/2022/06/dao-legal-framework-part-1.pdf

16. Page, K.L., Adel Elmessiry, A.E.: Global research decentralized autonomous organization (GR-DAO): a DAO of global researchers. In: International Conference on Cryptography and Blockchain (CRBL) (2021)

17. Mazur, J., Serafin, M.: Stalling the state: how digital platforms contribute to and profit from delays in the enforcement and adoption of regulations. Comp. Polit. Stud. 001041402210896 (2022). https://doi.org/10.1177/00104140221089651

18. Brummer, C.J., Seira, R.: Legal wrappers and DAOs. SSRN Electron. J. (2022). https://doi.org/10.2139/ssrn.4123737

19. Mienert, B.: How can a decentralized autonomous organization (DAO) be legally structured? Legal Revolutionary J. LRZ (2021)

20. Rosenberg, A.: Getting down with DAOs: decentralized autonomous organizations in bankruptcy. Am. Bankruptcy Inst. J. **41**(7), 12–51 (2022)

21. Larson, D.A.: Designing and implementing a state court ODR system: from disappointment to celebration. J. Disp. Resol. 77 (2019)

22. Jacobson, A.: Tennessee court pilots new ODR platform to mediate medical debt disputes. https://www.abajournal.com/magazine/article/tennessee-court-pilots-new-odr-platform-to-mediate-medical-debt-disputes
23. Minn, K.T.: Towards enhanced oversight of" self-governing" decentralized autonomous organizations: case study of the DAO and its shortcomings. NYU J. Intell. Prop. Ent. L. **9**, 139 (2019)
24. Sims, A.: Decentralised autonomous organisations: governance, dispute resolution and regulation. Dispute Resolut. Regul. (2021)
25. Ganado, M., Ellul, J., Pace, G.J., Tendon, S., Wilson, B.: Mapping the future of legal personality (2020)
26. Kaal, W.A.: Reputation as capital-how decentralized autonomous organizations address shortcomings in the venture capital market. Available at SSRN 3962614 (2021)

i-Bond: A Next Generation Bond's Issuing Service System

Ji Liu[1,2] , Zheng Xu[3], Yilin Sai[2], Yanmei Zhang[4], Dong Yuan[1], and Shiping Chen[1,2(✉)]

[1] School of Electrical and Information Engineering, The University of Sydney, Darlington, Australia
shiping.chen@data61.csiro.au
[2] CSIRO DATA61, Sydney, Australia
[3] Shenzhen Institute of Information Technology, Shenzhen, China
[4] Central University of Finance and Economics, Beijing, China

Abstract. To address the issues of the bond market's low transparency, information disclosure efficiency, and rating's ability to reveal risks, this paper proposes a blockchain-based bond primary market issuance service system, for companies to issue bonds efficiently at low cost. This paper presents the architecture design of the next-generation decentralised bond issuance service system. In addition, this paper also presents a new bond issuance bidding mechanism. Through the two-dimensional auction, the collusion between bond issuers has significantly been reduced, and the hidden danger of market manipulation has been eliminated. A prototype system was built on Hyperledger for proof of concept and performance evaluation.

Keywords: Blockchain · Fintech · Defi · Exchange · Primary financial market

1 Introduction

The low transparency of the bond market and the asymmetric information disclosure system have been impacted the bond market for a long time, which affects the high-quality development of the bond market [1]. As a distributed network system, blockchain technology has the characteristics such as tamper-proof, transparent, open, anonymousness, and verifiable execution, etc. It is inherently consistent with the current limitations for the sustainable development of the bond market, which can provide new technical solutions to the limitations of alleviating the growth of the bond market.

The authors have conducted an empirical study to investigate the rules of primary financial market in practice, which adopted a hybrid method combining interviews and online surveys [2]. The results further confirmed some important issues facing the primary bond issuing market, which are asymmetric information and low transparency. As a fellow-up of the previous work, this paper presents a design and prototype of a blockchain-based bond issuing system to address the above challenges in the bond issuing market.

S. Chen et al. (Eds.): ICBC 2022, LNCS 13733, pp. 29–47, 2022.
https://doi.org/10.1007/978-3-031-23495-8_3

The application of blockchain in the bond market can divide into two types [3]: (1) using alliance chain technology to optimise the bond issuance process, improve efficiency and reduce costs; (2) adopting public chain technology to implement bond issuance and trading. In traditional online transactions, the parties have their ledgers, and transaction records are not interoperable. However, each party involved in a transaction has its ledger in a standard visible network to see various historical records with blockchain technology. In this way, a reliable database with tamper-proof, open, and transparent capabilities is required. Specifically, adopting blockchain technology to issue bonds is reflected in three aspects.

(1) Reducing the risk of information asymmetry in the bond issuance process. The blockchain uses distributed ledger technology, and the information on the chain is recorded in the entire network in real-time, which reduces the risk of single-node accounting failure and helps ensure information security.
(2) Reducing the cost of bond issuance and improving the efficiency of bond issuance. Smart contracts can automatically execute bond issuance, automate complex business processing procedures, reduce manual intervention, and reduce manual operation costs. In addition, the completion of agreement signing certification on the blockchain can potentially replace the current offline paper agreement process and improve the efficiency of agreement signing.
(3) It is helpful for post-audit and management. Information related to bond issuance is recorded on the blockchain in a form that cannot be tampered with, which facilitates the retrospective verification of the bond issuance process in the future and reduces the workload of data verification. In addition, the information on the chain can automatically generate credible reports and statistics as needed to facilitate post-transaction management. In this paper, the contributions of our research are as follows:

- We developed a set concrete requirement from our previous experiment study, used to guide our design.
- We designed a new mechanism of bond issuing by adopting decentralised system.
- We developed a decentralised bond issuing service system and we conduct evaluation testing on its performance.

2 Requirement Analysis

2.1 Traditional Bond Market

Traditional bond issuance process usually involves several participants: issuers, investment banks, distributors, rating agencies, audit agencies, law firms, evaluation companies, etc. The traditional process can be summarized as shows in Fig. 1.

(1) The issuer needs to find one or more investment banks to organize the entire bond issuance, and then the selected investment banks recommend some distributors to better conduct bond sales services.
(2) Subsequently, the issuer needs to hire a law firm, audit firm, rating agency and other tripartite institutions to analyse the issuer's solvency.

(3) After all institutions have performed due diligence and issued the required reports, the investment bank will submit all the materials to the regulation institutions to apply for bond issuance.

(4) After approval by the exchange, the investment bank will lead all distributors to issue bonds.

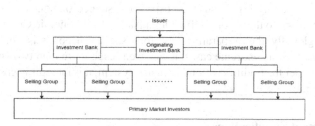

Fig. 1. A Traditional bond issuance process. Traditional bond issuance process

2.2 Limitations on Traditional Bond Issuance Process

Due to a lack of standardization, information asymmetry, fraud, and high cost on due diligence, the primary financial market has developed into a highly fragmented ecosystem structure. With the increasing development of the securities market, higher requirements are being placed on transaction costs, transaction efficiency, and transaction transparency. The cumbersome nature of such a business process cannot meet the needs of investment and financing entities. Even though industry and academia have attempted to change this status quo, no significant changes have been noticed [3]. Without solving the challenges listed above, it is difficult to optimize the infrastructure of the primary financial market.

The asymmetric information and low transparency issues in the financial market can be reflected in high bond issuance costs. Bond issuance costs mainly refer to the debt financing costs of a company. Issuance costs generally relatively high and cannot be omitted when calculating the cost of capital. Specifically, bond issuance costs include the lead underwriter and underwriting syndicate fees, other intermediary agency fees (including accounting firm fees, credit rating agency fees, law firm fees, asset evaluation fees (if any), and regulatory bank fees (such as Yes)) etc.

The underwriting expense of bond issuance has a certain proportional relationship with the financing scale. The underwriting fee rate of certain types of bonds is clearly stipulated by the relevant regulatory agencies, and there are also some different types of bonds with different costs. The relevant regulatory agencies have not issued guiding fee rate guidelines. The specific lead underwriters and underwriting group fee collection standards can be referred to for certain types of bonds. Normally, the lead underwriter and underwriting syndicate fees are paid after the bond issuance. The average underwriting fee for investment grade bond and junk bond are 0.7% and 1.2% in recent years [4].

There are extra intermediary agency fees in the market. Other intermediaries for bond issuance mainly include accounting firms, credit rating agencies, law firms, asset appraisal companies (if any) and regulatory banks (if any). These fees are the fees that need to be paid when issuing securities due to hiring the above-mentioned intermediary agencies to deal with issues related to the issuance.

Besides, if the issuer's credit rating is not high enough, to reduce the coupon rate of corporate bonds, it can pay for additional guarantors to increase the credit rating of corporate bonds. At this time, guarantee premium needs to be considered, it is range from 1% to 5% of total issue amount [4].

In addition to paying high issuance costs, the issuance of bonds must also consider time. According to the report of The Organisation for Economic Co-operation and Development, globally, the preparation time for issuance of bonds is usually not less than 5.5 months. In some extreme cases, it can even reach more than two years [5].

Therefore, under the traditional bond issuance system, it is incredibly costly in terms of money and time.

2.3 Requirement Specifications

Based on the content above, we designed the following system with blockchain technology as the core to solve the issues mentioned. In the proposed system, the issuance process can be divided into three steps: the submission of legal documents before the issuance, the auction of bonds at the time of issuance, and the supervision of funds after the issuance.

i-Bond will replace the underwriter to complete the bond sale responsibilities. Therefore, we can simplify actors as: third-party institutions, investors, and issuing companies. The core functions of the system will also be changed. The changed functions are uploading, bidding, bidding, settlement, and supervision. The system includes the following features:

R1. The platform consists of three types of users. Bond issuers and investors are the main interaction objects of the system. Third-party institutions only need to submit relevant legal documents before bond issuance.

R2. Before the bond issuance, third-party institutions need to submit documents such as guarantee letters, financial statements, credit ratings, and legal certifications. These documents will be stored in the shared repository for investors to review.

R3. After the relevant documents are ready, the issuer needs to initiate pricing and auction successively so that investors can evaluate and bid on them.

R4. The Investors can participate after receiving the news of pricing and auction if they are interested in investing. It is worth noting that in the auction link, investors need to mortgage the corresponding property before participating in the price.

R5. The initial auction price will be setup by the system, and it's calculated according to the market trend.

R6. Investors who have win the bid will have the right to purchase a corresponding amount of bonds.

With blockchain-based bond issuing system, the online bond issuance bookkeeping process is standardized, intelligent, and transparent with a blockchain-based bond issuing system. The system is based on blockchain technology to design smart contracts for bond businesses and ensure credible sharing of information through a consensus mechanism. On the one hand, it realizes the on-chain certificate deposit. Key information such as bond details during the bond issuance process is uploaded to the chain in real-time to realize distributed bookkeeping. On the other hand, it realizes the grouping on the chain. After the underwriting group is formed, the system will use the CA certificates of each participant to complete the group signature verification on the blockchain layer one by one.

3 Architecture Design

The system design is based on the core concept of parallel split [6] and horizontal expansion [7] at the service architecture level. It splits services according to business functions to achieve loosely coupled parallel operation of the system. At the same time, through a horizontal expansion and fault-tolerant recovery mechanism, the new services can be quickly deployed and released in grayscale, which improves the agility of the system. At the level of process construction, the system realizes multi-role, sub-authority online interaction, promotes paperless and online operations, and reduces the number of manual operations. In addition, multi-dimensional monitoring of the bond purchase process facilitates the real-time presentation of issuance dynamics.

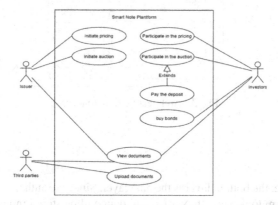

Fig. 2. Key roles in i-Bond.

Figure 2 demonstrates the overall use case diagram of the i-Bond. In the system, there are three organizations of users, called the Issuer, Investor and Third Party. All of whom can register and log in to their own account type. Aside from account registration and sign in, Third Party users are also able to view and upload files to the blockchain. Issuer users can view pricing submitted by the Investor users, as well as the bidding information. Investor users can submit pricing and bidding, as well as pay for their biddings. Based on the above-designed functionalities, there are four layers in the system. Figure 3 shows the architecture of i-Bond and how different components interact with each other.

This system is mainly composed of two layers: presentation layer and business layer. There are three target users in the system: issuer, investor, and third-party organization. The display layer interacts with the target users, which can provide users with all operations related to bond issuance. All users have the access to the presentation Layer. The front-end users can issue and trade bonds, set bidding, upload files, download files, and use the wallet in this layer.

The front-end application will obtain or transfer the required data to the business layer through the API. With the Hyperledger Fabric API, the front-end of the system can interact with the smart contract stored in the blockchain network at the business layer. Smart contracts are deployed on the Hyperledger in the data layer, and the system relies on it to maintain the operation of the entire program. Smart contracts can manage trading and clearing instructions for account holders, e.g., deposit and withdraw from the user's wallet, logging in or out, uploading files accordingly, etc.

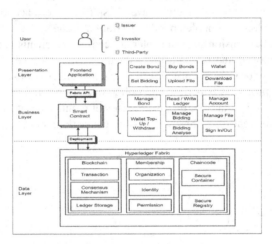

Fig. 3. Architecture of i-Bond.

3.1 Data Layer

In this architecture, the bottom layer is the data layer. Since the authors use Hyperledger Fabric as a platform to develop the project, all data will be stored in Hyperledger. The structure diagram of Hyperledger includes block management, member management, and Chaincode management, which means a high level of data security.

This project uses the latest version of Hyperledger Sect. 2.3, which can make progress not hindered by the defects of the old version and ensure that the project will not be required to update in a short time due to the rapid upgrading of technology. The system has a channel to deploy smart contracts when building Hyperledger. All transactions and records in the system are transmitted through this channel. In addition, three organizations were added to the channel when creating network, representing three different identities of issuer, investor, and third parties in the system. Each organization generates a CA server that issues certificates for all users in the organization to verify that new users added are valid users. Each newly joined user (peer) generates an MSP (Member Service Provider) that provides authentication when conducting transactions. Therefore, the system can also automatically identify the current user's identity through this mechanism and provide related services.

3.2 Business Layer

The business layer is above the data layer. The business layer is mainly implemented by smart contracts written in Javascript. Javascript is selected as the programming language of chaincode, as it is the most popular language in writing smart contracts compared with all other languages. In this project, all business logic (e.g., bidding management, bidding analysis, bond quote, document management) will be processed through smart contracts, and the necessary data will be written into the ledger and stored in the blockchain.

Smart contracts are the core of communication between the system and the blockchain. The storage method of data in Hyperledger consists of key-value pairs. After the smart contract gets the parameters returned by the system, it will calculate and store the necessary data in the blockchain.

Hyperledger provides three primary operations: put, get, and delete, which are sufficient to meet all our requirements for data storage and modification. The project's smart contract is mainly composed of two parts: TokenERC20Contract and SmartNote. The authors adopted the ERC-20Token standard regarding currency transactions to make the system's currency management and transaction processes more standardized. In order to meet the ERC-20 standard, the system implements many methods declared in its interface, such as totalSupply, transfer, balanceOf, approve, etc. After perfecting these methods, the system can get a complete currency transaction method. The SmartNote contract is mainly used to provide business services for the system. It covers many functions such as bond management, bidding management, document management, etc.

The system will generate a Transaction ID as the user's id when logging in to the system. The data security level is high since the blockchain obtains the Transaction ID through a series of algorithms such as hash. For security reasons, not only the user ID but also the Bond ID and File ID, we use Transaction ID as their unique identifier. However, these transaction IDs are often very long due to Hash calculations, and the readability is very poor.

Therefore, the authors have added the name attribute to Bond and File separately. When the user queries and browses the bond, the name will be used for identification, and only the internal processing of the system will select the Transaction ID as the identification code. This dramatically improves the system's ease of use and makes it easier for users to find and remember a bond.

3.3 Presentation Layer and User Layer

The top layer of the architecture is the display layer. JavaFx is chosen for the UI section. As JavaFX has its UI component library and runs in the Java virtual machine, the entire system can maintain the same UI interface no matter which system it runs in. Since it can obtain the current user's identity when the system is started, the system can omit the login interface and jump directly to the organisation's interface (Issuer, Investor or Third Party) to which the user belongs. In addition, the system can use the API and SDKs provided by Fabric to call smart contracts to achieve data interoperability between Java and Javascript.

The system needs to use the Gateway class in the SDK to establish a connection with the blockchain and then use the getNetwork() method to find the channel to which the current system belongs when the frontend needs to call the contract.

Finally, using the getContract() method to obtain the required smart contract, and then passing in the parameters and the name of the contract method to be called in the evaluateTransaction() method so that a call to the smart contract can be completed.

3.4 System Flow Design

Figure 4 shows the Business flowchart for this project. A brief description lists below:

(1) Third-party organizations submit relevant legal documents in the system
(2) Interested investors review and analyse these documents
(3) The issuer initiates the first round of pricing contracts
(4) Investors give the corresponding price for the bond based on their analysis, and the system will calculate a price range by itself
(5) The issuer initiates the second round of bidding contracts
(6) Investors pay a deposit for bidding, and the deposit will be returned after the bidding is over
(7) The winning investor buys bonds

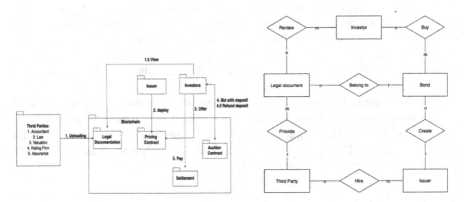

Fig. 4. Business flow chart.   **Fig. 5.** System E-R diagram.

3.5 Model Design

3.5.1 E-R Diagram Design

The E-R diagram clearly shows the attributes of the data objects and the connections between the data objects. Through the E-R diagram, we can more directly understand the possible interactions of the various objects in the entire system and the attributes they need. Here we select Account and Bond as the representatives of the entities for description.

The account contains 6 attributes: ID, Name, Balance, Bonds, E-mail and Type. Balance records the funds held by the account. All funds in this system will be managed through ERC20Token. Type is used to distinguish whether the account belongs to Issuer, Investor or Third Party. Bond contains 10 attributes. Advertised records whether the bond needs to be placed in the front of the list; Rate records the interest rate range of the bond in the auction; Files records all file IDs related to the bond.

E-R diagram of the entire system is shown in Fig. 5. An Issuer can create multiple bonds and hire multiple third-party agencies to provide legal documents for them. An Investor can view multiple documents and purchase multiple bonds. Each bond can have multiple legal documents, and each legal document can only belong to one bond.

3.5.2 Data Model Design

As Hyperledger's data storage method is limited to the storage of key-value pairs, it is impossible to design a database like a traditional project. The following modes are used to clarify the required attributes of an object:

Table 1. Account model table.

a) Account model	
field	Type
ID	String
Name	String
Balance	Double
RelatedBonds	String[]
E-mail	String

Table 2. Bond model table

b) Bond model	
field	Type
ID	String
Name	String
ownerId	Double
amount	String[]
price	String

(*continued*)

Table 2. (*continued*)

b) Bond model	
field	Type
rate	String
interest	Int
tpId	String[]
status	String
advertised	Boolean
endTime	Date
files	String[]
Bids	String[]

Table 3. File model table

c) File model	
field	Type
ID	String
Name	String
relatedBond	String
Content	String

4   Issuance Mechanism and Auction Algorithm Design

According to the theoretical models of [24, 25 and 26], the issuance mechanism of the bond primary market is discussed.

4.1   Market Participants

Market participants involved in bond issuance mainly include:

(1) Financing party (sell-side)
       The financier plans to issue a certain number of bonds for financing. The total amount of financing is Q, and the face value of the bonds is v^t. Before issuing bonds, the financier will select an underwriter and entrust the underwriter to organize the public bidding and issuance of bonds.
(2) Investors (buy-side)
       There are potential bidders amount $n(n \geq 2)$ in the market, and any bidder $i(i = 1, 2, \cdots, n)$ has an appraisal value v_i of the bond, and the appraisal value of each other is kept secret. The bidder i has a quasilinear utility function:

$$U_i(q_i, v_i) = u_i(q_i, v_i) + e_i \tag{1}$$

where, q_i is the number of bonds that won the bid, and e_i represents other costs. It is assumed that the utility function is a quadratic function $u_i(q_i, v_i) = v_i q_i - 0.5\alpha q_i^2$, α is used to measure the convexity of the utility function, which reflects the risk aversion of the bidders. The bidder's utility function is $mv(q_i, v_i) = v_i - \alpha q_i$. After the issuing of bonds, the bonds will be re-priced through transactions in the secondary market. At this time, bidders who hold the same amount of bonds will face the same market value, that is $v_i = v$. The strategy b_i of bidder i is a function of demand and value, which is $b_i(v_i, q_i) : \mathbb{R}_+^2 \to \mathbb{R}_+$.

(3) Platform (exchange)

The platform signs an underwriting agreement with the financier to provide services for bond issuance, which mainly includes formulating issuance rules and organizing the issuance process but does not participate in actual transactions. In addition, bonds issued on the platform are standardized products. Standardization can be understood as splitting bonds into equal Q parts, corresponding to the size of financiers issuing bonds. According to the Bayesian Nash equilibrium, starting from the maximization of the overall benefit, the mean number of bonds per bidder is $\overline{Q} = Q/n$, where the joint distribution function of $\overline{Q}$ and the face value v of the bond is $F(\overline{Q}, v)$.

4.2 Bidding and Issuance Mechanism

4.2.1 Bidding Process

The bidding process adopts a sealed quotation, and the bidder directly reports the assessed value of the bond (according to the bond pricing principle, each corresponds to a quotation rate) and the number of bids on the platform. Specifically, any bidder's offer consists of a series of "price-quantity". The timing of the bidding game is as follows:

Step1: The platform announces the bidding rules. The platform organizes the bidding process, announces the bidding rules, mainly including reserved price (or interest rate), configuration rules and payment rules, etc., and the bidding begins.

Step2: Investors bid. Investors make quotations after understanding the bidding rules, and the quotations are composed of a series of "price-quantity", that is the bidding strategy function $b_i(v_i, q_i)$.

Step3: Transaction and payment. The platform sorts the investors' quotations from high to low (or from low to high bidding rates), and wins the bids in turn, until the scale of the financing plan of the financier is met. When determining the equilibrium issue price v^e, the platform will add up the bidders (that is $v_i \geq v_0$, bidders who satisfy $r_i \leq r_0$) that satisfy the financier's reservation price in advance (v_0, the corresponding reservation interest rate is r_0) to obtain the total market demand. According to the principle of equal supply and demand $Q = \sum_i q_i(v^e)$, the equilibrium price (corresponding equilibrium interest rate r^e) is determined, which v^e is generally greater than or equal to the reservation price v_0 given by the financing party in advance. Then, configure and pay accordingly according to the bidding rules, and the bidding ends.

4.2.2 Issuance Mechanism

The issuance mechanisms commonly used in the bond issuance market include the Dutch issuance mechanism and the American issuance mechanism. When the Dutch issuance mechanism is adopted, the winning bidder subscribes for the number of bonds that are awarded at the same price (usually the lowest price of all winning bids, that is, the highest winning interest rate). When the American-style issuance mechanism is adopted, the winning bidders subscribe for the number of bonds won at their respective quoted prices (or the weighted average of the winning prices, that is, the weighted average winning rate). Considering that most of the bonds in the market currently use the Dutch issuance mechanism, this paper focuses on the Dutch issuance mechanism, allocation rules and payment rules. The specific provisions are as follows:

Configuration rules: bidders whose bids exceed the equilibrium price will win the bid, and the winning bidder will obtain the quantity corresponding to the equilibrium price, which is $q_i^e = q_i(v^e) = \{q : b_i(q, v) \geq v^e\}$.

Payment Rules: The winning bidder will pay all the winning bond quantities at the equilibrium price, with a total payment of $pay_i^{DBM} = q_i^e \times v^e$.

4.2.3 Equilibrium Price of Bidders

It is assumed that the game of all parties in the bidding process is a game of incomplete information, and its corresponding equilibrium is a Bayesian Nash equilibrium. The expected utility of each investor is maximized given the probability distribution of investor and other participants' choices ("winners"/"not winners"), so that no player is willing to change its behaviour or strategy. Based on the above assumptions, define the investor's return function as $U(q_i, v_i) - pay_i$, and the investor's expected return as $ER(q_i(v_i))$, then the investor's expected return is maximized as

$$\max ER(q_i(v_i)) = \Pr ob[b(q_i, v_i) \geq v^e] \times E[U(q_i, v_i) - pay_i | b(q_i, v_i) \geq v^e] \quad (2)$$

where, $\Pr ob[b(q_i, v_i) \geq v^e]$ represents the probability of the investor winning the bid, and $E[U(q_i, v_i) - pay_i | b(q_i, v_i) \geq v^e]$ represents the conditional expected return of the investor winning the bid. Based on the linear Bayesian Nash equilibrium model [24–26] the investor's equilibrium quotation is a linear function of demand and value, Specifically, at equilibrium, given that other investors adopt a linear quotation strategy, an investor using a linear quotation is a weakly dominant strategy. Define the supply function faced by the investor:

$$S(\overline{Q}, q_i, v_i) = n\overline{Q} - \sum_{j \neq i} q_j(v_j) \quad (3)$$

From the perspective of marginal utility, the equilibrium price is the price at which the investor's demand is equal to its supply, which is $q_i(v^e) = S_i(v^e)$. On this basis, the inverse supply function faced by investors i is $p(\overline{Q}, q_i, v_i) = c(q_i, v_i) + k_i S_i$, where p is the bond price; $c(q_i, v_i)$ is the intercept term, and its distribution function is expressed as $G(\bullet)$ (the probability density function is $g(\bullet)$), which can be obtained $k_i(k_i \geq 0) = \partial v^e / \partial q_i, \partial c(q_i, v_i) / \partial q_i < 0$ by $F(\overline{Q}, v)$.

Under the Dutch issuance mechanism, the winning bidder purchases the bond shares obtained at a uniform equilibrium price. According to the maximization expression of expected revenue of the winning bidder, the first-order condition for maximizing expected revenue is obtained, that is, marginal utility and marginal cost are equal:

$$v_i - \alpha q_i = p_i + k_i q_i \tag{4}$$

where the left side of the equation is the investor's marginal utility. The right side of the equation is the investor's marginal cost (or marginal expenditure), p_i represents the price of an additional unit of the winning bond, and $k_i q_i$ represents that the high quotation may lead to an increase in the equilibrium price, thereby increasing the price of the winning bond. From the above Eq. (4), the investor's optimal quotation function can be obtained as:

$$q_i = \frac{v_i - p_i}{k_i + \alpha} \tag{5}$$

To get the investor's optimal value q_i, it is necessary to obtain the optimal value k_i^e in the equilibrium state. In the equilibrium state, other investors $j(j \neq i)$ adopt the optimal quotation strategy of the above equations, and this time $k_j(j \neq i)$ becomes $k_j^e (j \neq i)$.Substitute Eq. (5) into the market clearing condition $q_i = S_i = n\overline{Q} - \sum_{j\neq i} q_j(v_j)$ to obtain the investor's equilibrium quotation condition as:

$$p_i = v_i + \left(\sum_{j\neq i} \left(k_j^e + \alpha\right)^{-1} \right)^{-1} (q_i - n\overline{Q}) \tag{6}$$

Therefore,

$$k_i^e = \left(\sum_{j\neq i} \left(k_j^e + \alpha\right)^{-1} \right)^{-1} \tag{7}$$

It can be shown that in the case of $n > 2$, there is a unique and symmetric equilibrium solution for the system of equations formed by Eqs. (7). Solve to get:

$$k_i^e = k_j^e = \frac{\alpha}{\alpha - 2} \tag{8}$$

Substituting the above (8) into (5), the bidder's linear Bayesian Nash equilibrium bid function is obtained as:

$$q_i^e = \frac{n-2}{\alpha(n-1)}(v_i - p_i) \tag{9}$$

Further averaging the equilibrium quotation function (9), according to the market clearing conditions, the equilibrium quotation faced by investors is obtained as:

$$v^e = v_i - \frac{n-1}{n-2}\alpha\overline{Q} \tag{10}$$

Thus, $v^e < v_i - \alpha \overline{Q}$, the investor's equilibrium offer will be lower than its true marginal value for the bond.

The equilibrium price may be obtained through a specific algorithm while running the system in the future. At present, for the algorithms to solve the Nash equilibrium, there are mainly algorithms for finding stable fixed points in GANs (such as gradient descent, optimistic mirror descent, and simultaneous gradient descent), Symplectic Gradient Adjustment, Mean-Based Learning Algorithms, etc.

5 Tests and Analysis

We implemented our design and algorithms using Hyperledger blockchain technology, and we deployed the system onto Amazon Cloud for performance testing. The authors have used baseline test and stress test to evaluate the performance of the system. The performance of the server is tested in terms of response time and through-put. Response time is measured under a variety of circumstances. On the other hand, throughput is used to measure how many requests the server can handle in the given unit of time (normally second).

The testing environment shows below: AWS EC2 instance having 16 vCPUs, 3.3 GHz AMD EPYC 7R32 processors and 32 GB RAM was used to run the test benchmark platform. The AWS EC2 instance ran Ubuntu 20.04 LTS and peers, CA, orderer, and Caliper with Fabric release v2.3.0. Each component of the Hyperledger Fabric, including 3 peers, 1 orderer and 1 Certificate Authority (CA), was launched as a Docker container. The results were obtained by putting the network under a fixed load of 500 transactions (sending rate is adjusted to maintain 500 unprocessed txs in the network).

For write txs:

(1) AddIssuer, AddInvestor, and AddThirdparty add new acting parties into the system, the parameters (company name, contact detail, id, etc.) are randomly generated.
(2) Then SubmitBond is benchmarked because the operation depends on existing parties in the system (added in step 1). Party ids in the parameters are randomly picked from existing parties, while other parameters are randomly generated, such as bond id. Bond data model can be found in architecture section.
(3) Then StartFirstBidding, SubmitInterest, EndFirstBidding are benchmarked in order because the operations depend on existing bonds in the system (added in step 2). Bond ids/Party ids in the parameter are randomly picked from existing bonds/parties, while other parameters are randomly generated. (Algorithm for first bidding can be found in algorithm section.)
(4) Then StartSecondBidding, SubmitBid, EndSecondBidding are benchmarked in order (Algorithm for second bidding can be found in algorithm section). Bond ids/Party ids in the parameter are randomly picked from existing bonds/parties, while other parameters are randomly generated.

For read txs, ReadItem is the operation to obtain object by id. Ids for each object type are provided to the operation when benchmarking. The ids are picked randomly from existing objects created in step 1–4 above. Object types include Issuer, Investor,

Third-party, bond, interest, and bid. The test results show in Table 4. In summary, the server does offer high availability and reliability both write and read. The latency is acceptable. Moreover, throughput is enough to handle the workload.

Table 4. Test results.

	Throughput (TPS)	Latency (s)
AddIssuer	227.4	1.15
AddInvestor	214.9	1.23
AddThirdParty	230.4	1.1
SubmitBond	193.2	1.48
StartFirstBidding	208.5	1.28
SubmitInterest	185.3	1.56
EndFirstBidding	190.7	1.46
StartSecondBidding	203.3	1.33
SubmitBid	190.5	1.4
EndSecondBidding	179	1.54
ReadIssuer	447.3	0.01
ReadInvestor	442.3	0.01
ReadThirdParty	422.7	0.01
ReadBond	426.7	0.01
ReadInterest	424	0.01
ReadBid	433.2	0.01

6 Related Work

Exploring the application of blockchain technology to the issuance of bonds in the primary market can start from two aspects: bond pricing using digital currency, and bond contracts using smart contracts. At present, the main parties involved in the traditional bond issuance on the primary market include accounting firms, law firms, rating agencies, guarantee agencies, underwriters and other service agencies, and there is a lack of information sharing among these parties. Due to insufficient trust mechanisms, low cost of fraud, and easy collusion between service agencies and issuers, the information disclosed by issuers may have fraud, causing investors to suffer losses due to information asymmetry. Blockchain technology can price the currency from the bottom. Take precautions with respect to bond contracts.

6.1 Credit Analysis Research

After the use of blockchain technology to popularize digital currency, due to tamper-proof, the issuer's accounting system and cash flow system will be more transparent than it is now [8]. Credit risk information such as financial fraud, legal disputes, financial deterioration, and misappropriation of funds that investors are worried about can be monitored [9]. The quality of corporate information will be greatly improved, prompting corporate operations to focus more on the main business. With the introduction of blockchain technology, credit analysis research may be weakened, which also means that the role of service agencies in the future will be weakened, financial statement fraud can be eliminated technically, and the workload of credit rating agencies and accounting firms will be reduced [10]. The record of information on the blockchain has strongly promoted the formation of financial decentralisation and flattening [11].

6.2 Issuer Information Disclosure

In the current state, if an issuer has credit risk defaults, regulators, banks, and lead underwriters need to verify the flow of funds for pedestrians, which will cost huge manpower, material, and financial resources. By adopting blockchain technology, the immutability of data and the retention of decentralised nodes will greatly reduce audit costs and improve the timeliness of information disclosure [12].

Investors can also grasp information in a timely manner or get feedback from the issuer, helping functional agencies such as the debt committee to improve the efficiency of credit monitoring. In addition, with the application and maturity of blockchain technology, small and medium-sized enterprises with sound financial status may have more comprehensive qualifications than large enterprises that currently have bond issuance qualifications, thus playing the role of survival of the fittest [13]. The precise positioning of the issuer's qualifications is conducive to investor protection, improves the availability and allocation efficiency of funds for SMEs, and enables financial support for the real economy to be more effectively implemented [14].

6.3 The Application of Smart Bond Contracts

Smart contract was proposed by Nick Szabo in 1994 [15], and its essence is to use programs to intelligently process contract terms. However, due to the limitations of the technical conditions at the time, smart contracts have not been widely used. In recent years, the programmable, traceable, tamper-proof, and decentralised characteristics of blockchain technology have quickly promoted the development of smart contracts. Combined with the features of automatic execution and smart execution of smart contracts themselves, smart contracts can be naturally applied to financial scenarios [16].

Specific to the bond market, smart bond contracts can realize the connectivity of various markets by adding bond parameters (bond elements, legal text, pledge conditions, etc.) and using standardized codes in bond transactions to reduce the supervision costs of bond regulators or industry associations. At the same time, it will help reduce the corporate default rate and the cost of bond issuance, improve the bond issuance process, and promote a healthier development of the bond market [17].

6.4 Industry Practices

August 2015, the smart contract platform Symbiont announced the first issuance of "smart securities" in the Bitcoin blockchain [18]. In May 2018, the Russian Federation

Sberbank completed Russia's first block-based Chain of commercial bond transactions [19]. In October 2019, Deutsche Bank's first digital bond was successfully issued on the EOS blockchain [20]. In December 2019, Bank of China launched the first domestic bond issuance system based on blockchain technology [21]. In September 2020, the Singapore Stock Exchange announced on its official website a digital bond project that has just been completed [22]. In November 2020, China Construction Bank plans to sell digital bonds worth USD 3 billion on the blockchain based on Ethereum technology [23]. Although subsequent issuances are cancelled, it is quite symbolic of the use of blockchain technology for bond issuance.

7 Conclusion and Future Work

This paper mainly focuses on the issues faced by the practical application of blockchain in bond issuing. The involvement of blockchain in bond issue, trade and settlement will weaken the reliance on financial intermediaries. Bond issuers and investors can achieve self-certification through blockchain transactions and historical behaviours. Thus, they can gain trust from each other and trade freely without limitations from central system. It will help the bond issue market to decrease fraud and collusion. From the view of financial infrastructure, it will balance digital transaction efficiency, supervision efficiency, offline production relations, and social distribution patterns.

Theoretically, technologies such as blockchain should be fully utilized to explore further how to improve the digital trading mechanism of the bond market. Technically, there are still many problems in the current blockchain bond trading system worthy of further analysis and research:

(1) It is significant to extend the ring signature technology (multi-party authentication mechanism) proposed in this paper to other blockchain transaction systems. It maintains distributed ledger data jointly by nodes and must consider the issue of privacy leakage. It is necessary to use ring signature technology in other applications of blockchain to provide privacy protection.

(2) Research on consensus protocols with faster transaction processing speed is still an essential topic in the blockchain field. The demand for transactions processed by the blockchain transaction system will increase with the continuous development of network technology. Continuous improvement based on the consensus protocol proposed in this paper can increase the processing speed of the blockchain system in an open distributed network.

(3) Studying the specific details of the reward distribution scheme in the blockchain system is of great significance for maintaining the system's security. The consensus protocol proposed in this paper should share block rewards by members of the verification group, but this paper does not set a reward distribution scheme. The reward mechanism in the blockchain transaction system is an essential guarantee for motivating nodes to maintain blockchain data jointly.

References

1. Stiglitz, J.E.: Financial markets and development. Oxf. Rev. Econ. Policy **5**(4), 55–68 (1989)
2. Liu, J., Xu, Z., Zhang, Y., Dai, W., Wu, H., Chen, S.: Digging into Primary Financial Market: Challenges and Opportunities of Adopting Blockchain. arXiv preprint arXiv:2204.09544 (2022)
3. Mori, T.: Financial technology: Blockchain and securities settlement. J. Secur. Oper. Custody **8**(3), 208–227 (2016)
4. Manju, D.: The New Floor for Bond Underwriting Fees: $1. The Wall Street Journal (2018). https://www.wsj.com/articles/the-new-floor-for-bond-underwriting-fees-1-1514973603. Accessed 13 Jan 2022
5. Çelik, S., Demirtaş, G., Isaksson, M.: Corporate bond markets in a time of unconventional monetary policy. Paris: OECD Capital Market Series (2019). Accesed 3 July 2020
6. Zhang, F., Sun, H., Xu, L., Lun, L.K.: Parallel-split shadow maps for large-scale virtual environments. In: Proceedings of the 2006 ACM International Conference on Virtual Reality Continuum and its Applications, pp. 311–318 (2006)
7. Jenkins, W., Strauser, D.R.: Horizontal expansion of the role of the rehabilitation counselor. J. Rehabil. **65**(1), 4 (1999)
8. Kolehmainen, T., Laatikainen, G., Kultanen, J., Kazan, E., Abrahamsson, P.: Using blockchain in digitalizing enterprise legacy systems: an experience report. In: Klotins, Eriks, Wnuk, Krzysztof (eds.) ICSOB 2020. LNBIP, vol. 407, pp. 70–85. Springer, Cham (2021). https://doi.org/10.1007/978-3-030-67292-8_6
9. Hyvärinen, H., Risius, M., Friis, G.: A blockchain-based approach towards overcoming financial fraud in public sector services. Bus. Inf. Syst. Eng. **59**(6), 441–456 (2017)
10. Garg, P., Gupta, B., Chauhan, A.K., Sivarajah, U., Gupta, S., Modgil, S.: Measuring the perceived benefits of implementing blockchain technology in the banking sector. Technol. Forecast. Soc. Chang. **163**, 120407 (2021)
11. Ye, S., Zeng, J.: The mechanism and strategy of blockchain technology driving the development of supply chain finance. In: 2021 International Conference on Social Sciences and Big Data Application (ICSSBDA 2021), pp. 207–211. Atlantis Press (2021)
12. Yu, T., Lin, Z., Tang, Q.: Blockchain: the introduction and its application in financial accounting. J. Corp. Account. Finance **29**(4), 37–47 (2018)
13. Joo, M.H., Nishikawa, Y., Dandapani, K.: ICOs, the next generation of IPOs. Managerial Finance (2019)
14. Blémus, S., Guégan, D.: Initial crypto-asset offerings (ICOs), tokenization and corporate governance. Capital Markets Law J. **15**(2), 191–223 (2020)
15. Szabo, N.: Formalizing and securing relationships on public networks. First Monday (1997)
16. Cong, L.W., He, Z.: Blockchain disruption and smart contracts. Rev. Finan. Stud. **32**(5), 1754–1797 (2019)
17. Tian, Y., Adriaens, P., Minchin, R.E., Chang, C., Lu, Z., Qi, C.: Asset tokenization: a blockchain solution to financing infrastructure in emerging markets and developing economies. ADB-IGF Spec. Working Pap. Ser. Fintech Enable Dev. Investment Financ. Incl. Sustain. (2020)
18. Smart securites. (2015). https://www.symbiont.io. Accessed 13 Jan 2022
19. Sberbank carries out Russia's first payment transaction using blockchain technology. (2017). https://www.sberbank.ru/en/press_center/all/article?newsID=9f676571-5219-4cfb-bbb7-c9c6e1de983a&blockID=1539&regionID=77&lang=en&type=NEWS. Accessed 13 Jan 2022
20. Deutsche Bank bond tokenized on the EOS mainnet. (2019). https://www.eosgo.io/news/deutsche-bank-bond-tokenized-on-the-eos-mainnet. Accessed 13 Jan 2022

21. Bank of China Issues $2.8B in Bonds for Small Businesses Using Blockchain Tech. (2019). https://au.finance.yahoo.com/news/bank-china-issues-2-8b-180500855.html. Accessed 13 Jan 2022
22. SGX, in collaboration with HSBC and Temasek, completes pilot digital bond for Olam International (2020). https://www.sgx.com/media-centre/20200901-sgx-collaboration-hsbc-and-temasek-completes-pilot-digital-bond-olam. Accessed 13 Jan 2022
23. Alun, J.: China Construction Bank unit raising $3 bln via blockchain bond. Nasdaq website (2020). https://www.nasdaq.com/articles/china-construction-bank-unit-raising-%243-bln-via-blockchain-bond-2020-11-10. Accessed 13 Jan 2022
24. Financing for Development: Issuance Mechanism Design for Local Government Bonds in China. **18**(04), 1489–1508 (2019). https://doi.org/10.13821/j.cnki.ceq.2019.03.15
25. Holmberg, P.: Supply function equilibria of pay-as-bid auctions. J. Regul. Econ. **36**(2), 154–177 (2009)
26. Wang, J.J., Zender, J.F.: Auctioning divisible goods. Econ. Theory **19**(4), 673–705 (2002). https://doi.org/10.1007/s001990100191

A UI/UX Evaluation Framework for Blockchain-Based Applications

Jeyakumar Samantha Tharani[✉], Dorottya Zelenyanszki, and Vallipuram Muthukkumarasamy

School of Information and Communication Technology, Griffith University, Brisbane, Australia
jeyakumar.samanthatharani@griffithuni.edu.au

Abstract. The decentralised nature and the traceability of multi-chain transactions increase the use of blockchain technology in various domains such as finance, supply chain, health, governance, and entertainment [1]. There remains a need for more studies about the usefulness of blockchain technology in different applications, particularly requiring an understanding of the effectiveness of blockchain adoption. There is also a need for providing standards for evaluating and measuring the User Interface (UI)/ User Experience (UX) functionalities. In fact, there are only a few studies that have evaluated the UI/UX aspects of the blockchain space. Appropriately evaluating the design of a UI will enable the enhancement of the UX and facilitates a deeper understanding of the usefulness of the technology. In this research, we propose a novel evaluation framework to measure the UI/UX aspects of blockchain-enabled applications based on the requirements, volume of data, and performance. We demonstrate the utility and usability evaluations of the framework through a case study of a visualisation tool for blockchain transactions. The outcome of the evaluation shows that due to the intrinsic nature of the blockchain the UI elements of its applications need special consideration in performance and responsiveness. These could enhance the potential use of this emerging technology and bring confidence among stakeholders to integrate that into their core business or daily life.

Keywords: UI/UX · Blockchain-based application · Evaluation · Framework · Software development lifecycle · Agile

1 Introduction

Blockchain is one of the most promising and emerging technologies. It can be used in several industries including healthcare, finance, logistics, construction management, and telecommunication. This technology is extremely powerful and has the ability to change the way we live, interact, do business and govern. It cannot, however, reach its full potential until stakeholders realise the benefit of using it appropriately. Among most users, blockchain technology is currently treated as an unknown or less understood and uncertain technology. At this stage, blockchain-based research and industrial application development mainly focus on the technical aspects of the applications and hardly pays attention to the user experience. This may result in an unsatisfactory user experience which could have a misleading effect on the overall usefulness of blockchain technology. This may lead to reduced levels of investment and/or involvement of the users and industries.

This highlights the need for proper consideration in the UI/UX evaluation of blockchain-based applications. An efficient design of UI will demonstrate and inform the users on how they could fully exploit the benefit of blockchain technology to achieve their goals effectively, efficiently and satisfactorily. This may then encourage the massive adaption of next-generation blockchain-based applications in suitable sectors.

Only a few studies in the literature incorporate UI elements in their blockchain-based applications such as smart health monitoring, Agri-food supply chain, distributed marketplace, and mobile application development. Even though only the works [4,8] considered and evaluated the UI/UX aspects by using users-based evaluation, they discovered that the involvement of users in the evaluation is lower in blockchain-based research than the non-blockchain-based ones. Also, more comprehensive research must be conducted from both technical and UI/UX aspects.

The evaluation of UI/UX in blockchain-based applications needs special consideration compared to traditional software applications. The design and development nature of blockchain-based applications has different structures and characteristics which may require an innovative approach in terms of design and evaluation of UI/UX. For example, UI elements related to the response time of the transaction and the volume of data have a deep, possibly unacceptable, effect on the usability of the application, which can lead to a problematic UX. The research related to UI/UX evaluation often considers the user experience after the implementation of the application [4,9]. For the best user interaction with the technical aspects ideally, it should focus from the beginning to the end of the whole development lifecycle. By considering these gaps this research propose, to the best of our knowledge, the first UI/UX evaluation framework for blockchain-based applications. This framework can evaluate the UI/UX of blockchain-based applications throughout the development lifecycle. The proposed novel framework incorporates the UI/UX evaluation in all three development phases such as requirement gathering, design and implementation, validation and testing.

The structure of the paper is as follows. Section 2 presents the related work in the context of UI/UX evaluation and elements. Section 3 describes an overview of the proposed UI/UX evaluation framework. Section 4 shows the implementation details of the visualisation tool for blockchain transactions. Sections 5 and 6 describe the evaluation process, and recommendations for the blockchain transaction visualisation tool respectively. Finally, Sect. 7 concludes the paper.

2   Related Works

This section discusses the related work based on the UI/UX evaluation, and the existing blockchain-based research connected to the UI/UX aspects.

Alomari et al. [2] presented multiple user studies that can be used to assess the usability and utility of a cyberlearning environment by using user interfaces and user experience evaluations. They proposed a UI/UX evaluation framework for the cyberlearning environment. This reference is considered a good starting point for our proposed UI/UX evaluation framework.

Hossain et al. [3], proposed a graphical user interface (GUI) for MultiChain blockchain to improve the involvement of people without any technical background. Their evaluation study showed that the integration of GUI increased the usability of the Multichain platform in different sectors such as financial, educational, medical, etc. They used user study-based evaluation to assess the usability of the proposed GUI in terms of effectiveness, efficiency, and satisfaction.

Jang et al. [4], conducted a study to identify the fundamental causes of problems that users encounter when they interact with blockchain technology. They used KDEX decentralised application to evaluate the usability. Their results concluded that a more user-centred design is necessary to enable the widespread use of decentralised applications. Also, the developers need to invest more effort in understanding UX when designing the DApps.

Rahman et al. [7], proposed a gesture-based smart home IoT health device to support the elderly or special-need people. The use case of blockchain technology in this research work only focused on secure data sharing and management. This proposed device has UIs to create and monitor smart home IoT devices. There is no specific UI design mentioned to monitor the blockchain use cases.

Tharatipyakul et al. [8], proposed and evaluated user interfaces for blockchain-based agri-food supply chain management. They prepared a survey to evaluate UI elements. The evaluation result concluded that the involvement of users in the evaluation is lower among blockchain-based researchers than the non-blockchain-based ones.

Tovanich et al. [9] conducted a detailed survey on blockchain data visualisations which can be used as a foundation to design visualisation for various types of blockchain networks. This study was conducted among practitioners and researchers in economics, computer science, and even public audiences. They provided the classification scheme to group visualizations based on five aspects: Target blockchains, blockchain data, task domains, target users, and visualization types.

The UI/UX evaluation for traditional applications mentioned in the literature does not pay more attention to the response time for loading UI elements and the traceability of the user's request outcomes. Whereas, the applications running on the blockchain network have special features such as validating transactions, and traceability of the digital asset. These features are highly correlated with the response time of the UI elements. When an application takes more time to load the UI element it loses the UX among the end-users [5,6]. Also, it needs

Table 1. Challenges in designing UI/UX evaluation framework

Challenges	Description
Limited attention on UI/UX aspects	Blockchain itself have limitations and challenges in terms of scalability, interoperability, and security and researchers mainly focus on those
Lack of system of knowledge	Hardly exists any guidelines, standards or proven processes for systematic design
The maturity level of blockchain technology	Limited understanding of new approaches needed for the implementation of UI for blockchain-related applications

a special UI design to show the movement of the digital asset. This facilitates a more clear understanding of the usefulness of blockchain technology among investors and end-users. In this proposed framework, evaluation of these aspects is considered as key elements. Also, this framework incorporates the knowledge level of different user groups as an evaluation measure of the UX.

2.1 Limitation and Challenges

This sub-section discusses the limitations and specific challenges of designing UI for blockchain-based applications. The previous research [8] highlights some of the challenges of the UI/UX, such as more focus on the technical elements than the usability aspect, lack of domain knowledge among the developers or designers, and the uncertainty of the blockchain and its elements becoming highly challenging to design specific UI elements for blockchain-based applications. Table 1 summarises the major challenges in the UI/UX aspects regarding the implementation of blockchain-based applications.

3 Proposed Framework

This section describes the proposed novel UI/UX evaluation framework to design user-friendly interfaces for blockchain-based applications and provides a guideline to measure the user experience.

3.1 Mapping

Blockchain-based application requirements should mainly be designed based on the features of the blockchain architecture. This includes mapping between the user requirements such as processes, limits, etc. and the elements of blockchain-based applications. It facilitates the identification of the real need for blockchain technology in the application requirements. Then only the developer can choose the suitable UI elements, preferably under the guidance of a UX specialist. This process offers a strong foundation for creating an effective concept plan for the implementation phase.

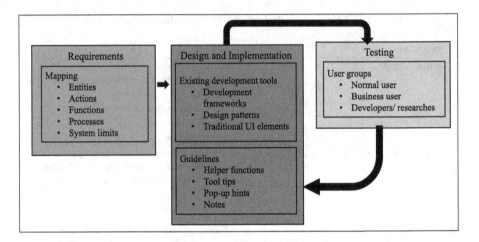

Fig. 1. Proposed UI/UX evaluation framework for blockchain-based application

3.2 Adopting Design Patterns and UI Elements

The usage of existing standardised UI elements will bring more confidence to both the designer and end users since they are already familiar with them. Therefore, it is recommended to use the existing UI elements, where possible, which are already used in traditional applications. However, as a result of the underlying uncertainty around blockchain technology, it is highly plausible that a new diverse approach may be required in future.

3.3 Developing Guidelines

The users often do not appreciate the value of the usage of the blockchain and find difficulties in understanding the functionalities. Adding guidelines and other helper elements (tooltip/ hints) to the user interface will enhance the user experience. A good example of this is an overview page with a detailed explanation of the application flow. This is essential, especially if they were designed for blockchain purposes. These guideline components are highly important for all users, but they are essential for new users who have no knowledge of this technology.

3.4 Identifying User Groups

The UI design highly depends on the identified target end-user group(s). We identify three categories of user groups that are possible in blockchain-based applications:

1. **Normal User:** The users without any kind of blockchain knowledge. The users belonging to this category are normally not interested in experiencing

the technical aspects of the blockchain-based application. The guideline components are highly important for this user group. It is potentially the key to creating a high level of user experience for them.

2. **Business User:** The business user can be an investor, an analyst or another type of business-related person who is seeking revenue from the use cases. The people who belong to this category might have some background knowledge. However, the level of understanding is probably limited and a certain percentage of people in this category also may not wish to be involved in the technological aspects. Guidelines and UI elements that reflect the traceability of the end-users actions can be useful for monitoring business-related elements.

3. **Developers and Researchers:** The users who are involved in the research work on the analysis of the blockchain network, or the developers who are working on the blockchain-related applications are considered in this category. The UI elements for these users need to consider mainly the technical aspects of blockchain technology.

To the best of our knowledge, this is a novel framework which incorporates the UI/UX evaluation from the beginning to the end of the development lifecycle. Also, the elements of the framework are structured by considering the key elements of the blockchain and the knowledge level of the participants as presented in Fig. 1. As we mentioned in the introduction, blockchain is an evolving technology. Most of its key elements are still under research in relation to real-world adoption. This status brings agile-based development to blockchain-based applications.

Our framework incorporate the agile development approach by revisiting the designing phase after receiving feedback from the end users. For example, Fig. 9 is an interface to check the result of the anomalous behaviour in a graph pattern. Earlier it was designed without the selection of classifiers. Then we incorporated classifier selection based on our end user suggestion. Now, the user can visualise the anomalous behaviour based on the selected classifiers prediction results.

4 Experimental Setup

This section captures the implementation details of the visualisation tool for blockchain transactions. The proposed UI/UX evaluation framework applies to this tool to determine the strengths and weaknesses of its UI/UX. This application is mainly designed for network engineers, forensic analysts, and investors who have an interest in the transaction details of the blockchain network.

Through this application, the end user can visualise various kinds of blockchain network elements in an interactive graphical view. They can examine the related information and features of the nodes and visualise the patterns of the normal and anomalous transaction nodes. The application follows a simple, minimised design and workflow. To start, the user can use the left-hand menu that can be seen in Fig. 2 to navigate to a certain part of the application. This menu also includes a list of blockchain networks so that the users can choose

Table 2. Technologies and specifications of the blockchain-based application

Category	Sotware/System Details
Operating system	Windows 10/ Linux 20.04.4 LTS
Front-end framework	NodeJs 16.x, VueJs3.0
Language	Python 3.7.x
Database	Neo4j graph database 1.4.x
Software framework	MVC
CPU and Memory	11th Gen Intel(R) Core(TM) i7-11850H & 32.0 GB

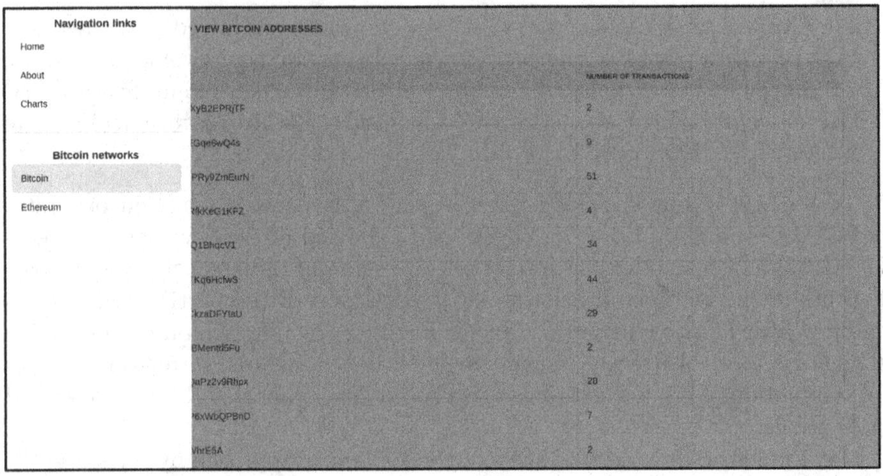

Fig. 2. Menu to select the blockchain network

their preferred blockchain to examine its behaviour. Table 2 represents the technologies and system specification details of our blockchain-based application.

5   Evaluation of the Proposed Framework on Blockchain-Based Application

This section explains the proposed UI/UX evaluation framework via measuring the UI/UX aspects of the analysis tool for blockchain transactions explained in Sect. 4. This evaluation process measures the appropriateness of the UI elements with the application requirements, and the usability aspects in terms of the mapping between the requirements and the UI elements, delay in rendering, and responsive view on different devices.

5.1   Mapping

This application is mainly designed to get experience and a deeper understanding of the blockchain's internal structure. Blockchain is a collection of blocks →

each block is a collection of transactions → each transaction associated with the wallet addresses. The flow of this application incorporates these aspects. The user first needs to select the blockchain network as in Fig. 2. Based on the selection they can visualise the wallet addresses involved in the network as in Fig. 3. After that, the user can click on the hyperlink associated with every address (presented in Fig. 4) to see the details of the transactions corresponding to the selected addresses. In Fig. 5 the transactions list view is presented using the table component.

The next phase of this application is graph visualisation. To visualise the transactions, the user can simply select the transaction using a checkbox as in Fig. 6 and then the action button labelled as 'V' can be used to redirect to the graph visualisation page. The graph visualisation can be viewed either 2D as in Fig. 7 or 3D as in Fig. 8.

The final phase of the application is the analysis and visualisation of the normal and anomalous graph patterns. To analyse the transaction(s), first, the user needs to select the transaction(s) and then click on the action button 'A' which will redirect the user to the analysis page. Then the user can select the machine learning classifier(s) as in Fig. 9 and visualise their results in the graph format. The graph representation of the analysis differentiates the normal nodes from the anomalous ones via different colour codes (under development). The graph representations are zoomable and movable which facilitates more interaction with the end users and the graph nodes.

Overall the mapping between the requirements, the UI element selection and the system flow was well designed.

5.2   Adopting Design Patterns and UI Elements

The UI elements used in this blockchain analysis tool adopt suitable existing, commonly used elements. The details of the UI elements and the requirements are stated in Table 3. Adopting the existing UI elements encourages the users to play around with this tool without the need for any additional knowledge.

Table 3. UI elements for the application requirements

Functional Requirement	UI Element
Select the blockchain network	Left-hand menu
Represent wallet address details	Table
Represent transaction details	Table
Select the transaction	Checkbox
Visualise the transaction	Graph library[a]
Page navigation/ redirection	Action button and left-hand menu

[a]https://github.com/zjfcool/vue-force-graph

5.3   Identifying User Groups

This application is mainly designed for network engineers, forensic analysts, and investors. The main intentions of these users are to get a deeper understanding of the blockchain's internal structure and visualise the normal and abnormal behaviours of its transactions. The flow of this tool well incorporates the internal structure of the blockchain and produces the analysis results in a graphical pattern. This design brings more understanding to the internal structure of the blockchain and its normal and abnormal behaviour in a user-friendly manner.

6   Recommendations

This section provides recommendations regarding UI/UX enhancement in the blockchain analysis tool. The existing system does not have any guidelines for the end users to guide them through the workflow of this application. During the testing, we encountered a delay in graph rendering when the number of nodes increased. To address this and similar issues, the application needs to incorporate helper functionalities (e.g.: timer, loading button, progress bar). An additional timer or a loading button is a simple user element but it can enhance the user experience and make them understand more about how the backend side of the system works.

BLOCKCHAIN UI TOOL >> VIEW BITCOIN ADDRESSES	
ADDRESS	NUMBER OF TRANSACTIONS
17TMc2UkVRSga2yYvuxSD9Q1XyB2EPRjTF	2
1DTE5x3Rjn2q75HjX6hiu8CQwEGqe6wQ4s	9
3KmK5z4CAvn3aL4Q8F2gWbhuPRy9ZmEurN	51
1C7FeXMf18mGrcF59DJTkmxnRfkKeG1KFZ	4
3PDtzkTnD1E7gB7peZ2prRyDxjQ1BhqcV1	34
3LLzycFNFh7mDsqRhfknfGBa6TKq6HcfwS	44
37m57HiP5rPceopgEWF9sM58CkzaDFYtaU	29
18x7PieotZcmMwYSaYbbV8X3zBMentd5Fu	2
3Gwz3yVmrGr5AqmUrAS8H2QQaPz2v9Rhpx	28
1Kcwserp7KqSMYBDe6Ra5alHP6xWbQPBnD	7
1GuPsTqJjib8t2idTaLwa95kRLtiWhrE5A	2

Fig. 3. List of wallet addresses in the blockchain network

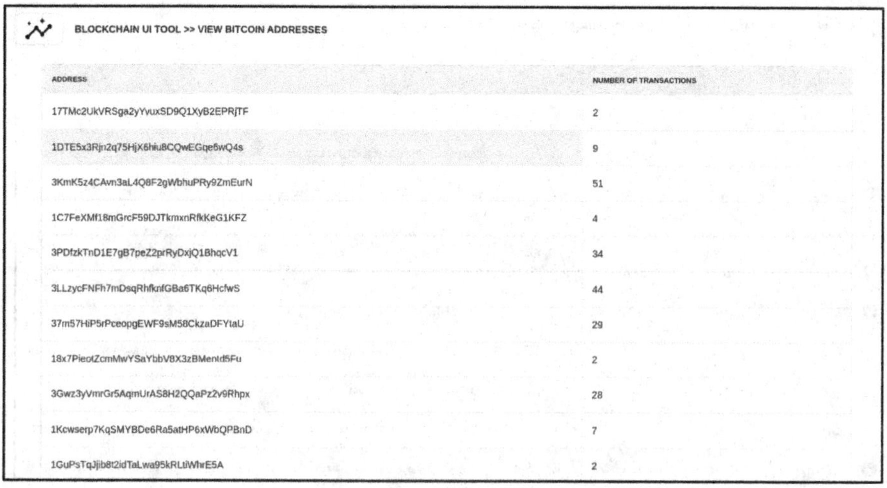

Fig. 4. Wallet addresses with hyperlink

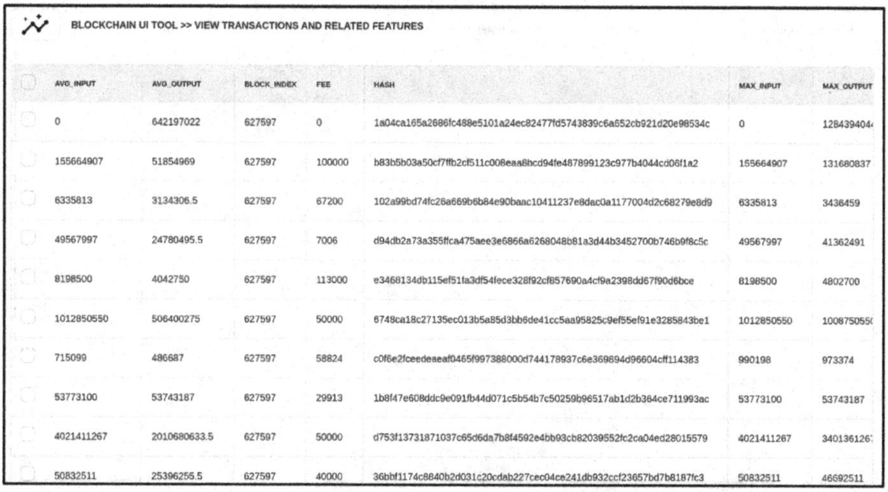

Fig. 5. List of transactions in a wallet address

BLOCKCHAIN UI TOOL >> VIEW TRANSACTIONS AND RELATED FEATURES

[V] [A]

	AVG_INPUT	AVG_OUTPUT	BLOCK_INDEX	FEE	HASH	MAX_INPUT	MAX_OUTPUT
☐	0	642197022	627597	0	1a04ca165a2686fc488e5101a24ec82477fd5743839c6a652cb921d20e98534c	0	128439404·
☑	155664907	51854969	627597	100000	b83b5b03a50cf7ffb2cf511c008eaa8bcd94fe487809123c977b4044cd06f1a2	155664907	131680837
☑	6335813	3134306.5	627597	67200	102a99bd74fc26a669b6b84e90baac10411237e8dac0a1177004d2c68279e8d9	6335813	3436459
☑	49567997	24780495.5	627597	7006	d94db2a73a355ffca475aee3e6866a6268048b81a3d44b3452700b746b9f9c5c	49567997	41362491
☑	8198500	4042750	627597	113000	e3468134db115ef51fa3df54fece328f92cf857690a4cf9a2398dd67f90d6bce	8198500	4802700
☐	1012850550	506400275	627597	50000	6748ca18c27135ec013b5a85d3bb6de41cc5aa95825c9ef55ef91e3285843be1	1012850550	100875055(
☑	715099	486687	627597	58824	c0f8e2fceedeaeaf0485f997388000d744178937c6e369894d96804cff114383	990198	973374
☐	53773100	53743187	627597	29913	1b8f47e608ddc9e091fb44d071c5b54b7c50259b96517ab1d2b364ce711993ac	53773100	53743187
☑	4021411267	2010680833.5	627597	50000	d753f13731871037c65d6da7b8f4592e4bb93cb82039552fc2ca04ed28015579	4021411267	340136126·

Fig. 6. Selection of transactions

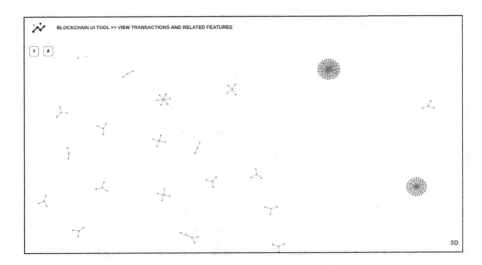

Fig. 7. Graph representation for transactions in 2D

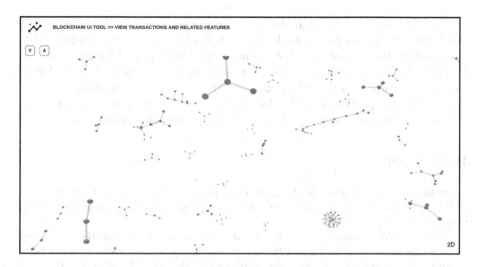

Fig. 8. Graph representation for transactions in 3D

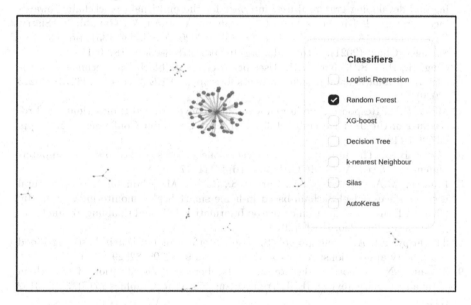

Fig. 9. Selection of different classifiers

7 Conclusion

This research work proposed a novel UI/UX evaluation framework for blockchain-based applications. We have tested this framework by evaluating the UI/UX elements of a blockchain transactions visualisation tool. Through this study, we identified that the UI/UX should be in consideration throughout the development life cycle of the blockchain-based application. This will enhance the usability and the maintainability of the system among the end-users and the developers. In our future work, the proposed framework will develop a theory based on the mental model of the users. The mental model aspects will be formulated via conducting surveys or testing among participants from different sector user groups, and the enhancement of the framework based on the feedback coming from the participants. We also aim to investigate the need for blockchain-specific UI elements which would be applicable to specific applications.

References

1. Al-Jaroodi, J., Mohamed,N.: Industrial applications of blockchain. In: 2019 IEEE 9th Annual Computing and Communication Workshop and Conference (CCWC), pp. 0550–0555 (2019)
2. Alomari, H.W., Ramasamy, V., Kiper, J.D., Potvin, G.: A user interface (UI) and user experience (UX) evaluation framework for cyberlearning environments in computer science and software engineering education. Heliyon **6**(5), e03917 (2020)
3. Hossain, T., Mohiuddin, T., Hasan, A.M.S., Islam, M.N., Hossain, S.A.: Designing and developing graphical user interface for the multichain blockchain: towards incorporating HCI in blockchain. In: Abraham, A., Piuri, V., Gandhi, N., Siarry, P., Kaklauskas, A., Madureira, A. (eds.) ISDA 2020. AISC, vol. 1351, pp. 446–456. Springer, Cham (2021). https://doi.org/10.1007/978-3-030-71187-0_41
4. Jang, H., Han, S.H., Kim, J.H.: User perspectives on blockchain technology: user-centered evaluation and design strategies for dapps. IEEE Access **8**, 226213–226223 (2020)
5. Miller, R.B.: Response time in man-computer conversational transactions. In: Proceedings of the 9–11 December 1968, Fall Joint Computer Conference, Part I, pp. 267–277 (1968)
6. Myers, B.A.: The importance of percent-done progress indicators for computer-human interfaces. ACM SIGCHI Bull. **16**(4), 11–17 (1985)
7. Rahman, M.A., Abualsaud, K., Barnes, S., Rashid, M., Abdullah, S.M.: A natural user interface and blockchain-based in-home smart health monitoring system. In: 2020 IEEE International Conference on Informatics, IoT, and Enabling Technologies (ICIoT), pp. 262–266. IEEE (2020)
8. Tharatipyakul, A., Pongnumkul, S.: User interface of blockchain-based agri-food traceability applications: A review. IEEE Access **9**, 82909–82929 (2021)
9. Tovanich, N., Heulot, N., Fekete, J.-D., Isenberg, P.: Visualization of blockchain data: a systematic review. IEEE Trans. Visual Comput. Graphics **27**(7), 3135–3152 (2021)

From Business-Level Specifications to Smart Contracts for Blockchain-Based Resource-Exchange Systems

Kushal Soni[✉] and Olga De Troyer

Computer Science Department, Vrije Universiteit Brussel, Brussels, Belgium
{Kushal.Soni,Olga.DeTroyer}@vub.be

Abstract. Blockchain technology allows to store data in a secure and decentralized manner and can provide true ownership to the owners of the data. Therefore, it could be a good solution for applications where this is required. Resource-exchange systems are such a type of application. To allow to easily set up such systems using blockchain technology, we have introduced a framework that allows to generate such applications. The use of the framework does not require programming or blockchain knowledge. The range of applications that can be generated with the framework are applications for the management and exchange of resources across organizations and their customers. In this paper, we present the generation of the smart contracts from high-level specifications. We explain the mapping from the high-level user concepts used to specify a use case onto the technical concepts used in blockchain and smart contracts technology. We explain the different types of contracts generated as well as their role and functionality. The exchange of resources by means of these smart contracts is illustrated with some examples. We also discuss the limitations and further work.

Keywords: Blockchain · Smart contract generation · Generic framework · Businesspeople · Resource exchange

1 Introduction

More and more businesses and organizations offer several digital services to their users. This implies the need for IT infrastructures, i.e., databases, to store and maintain related user data and/or resources. In general, this information is maintained and managed by the organization offering the service. As a result, users are lacking true ownership of their data and resources. Blockchain technology provides a novel approach to store data and could be a good solution to provide true ownership of data and resources to the users. With this technology, data is stored in a decentralized manner in a blockchain network, maintained by a group of computers and servers, called nodes. Full nodes keep a copy of the blockchain database, which consists of a series of linked blocks, each containing the transactions expressing operations that result in changes of data. The redundancy that is created in this way ensures the integrity of the data. Furthermore, the lack of an authority having the ownership of the database is one of the main advantages of a

© The Author(s), under exclusive license to Springer Nature Switzerland AG 2022
S. Chen et al. (Eds.): ICBC 2022, LNCS 13733, pp. 61–77, 2022.
https://doi.org/10.1007/978-3-031-23495-8_5

blockchain network, as it gives full control to the person owning the resource(s) [1–3]: ownership of resources can be stored on the blockchain and the logic of an application can be stored in smart contracts that are publicly verifiable. Smart contracts are pieces of program code that run under certain programmed conditions. Once deployed, the logic of the contracts cannot be changed [4].

In our research, we focus on services that businesses and organizations offer to allow customers, clients, or other types of users to earn/own resources. For instance, shops that allow customers to earn loyalty points, or organizations that award degrees or certificates to people. In addition, we consider the service of exchanging resources between different parties. For instance, in case of points earned in loyalty programs, a person may consume loyalty points in another shop than the one in which they were earned. In general, such sharing of loyalty points is less supported by companies. However, more and more we see such collaborations between businesses (e.g., Miles & More is one of the largest airline loyalty programs with a wide range of partners).

The aim of our research is to allow non-IT skilled people to set up a blockchain application for the management and exchange of resources, without the need to rely on programmers. To achieve this, we propose a framework that allows businesspeople to specify their use case in business terms using an easy-to-use web interface, and that subsequently generates the application including the smart contracts. Note that the framework could also be used by IT-companies to speed up the process of creating such applications. The framework was proposed in [5]. The web application that allows a non-IT skilled person to specify the requirements for a use case, has been described in detail in [6] and the generation process was briefly described in [7]. Here, we provide the details of the generation process of the smart contracts required for the deployment of the blockchain application.

In Sect. 2, we discuss related work. Section 3 briefly presents the framework. Section 4 discusses the generation of the smart contracts and illustrates the use of the smart contracts by means of some examples. Limitations and future work are discussed in Sect. 5, and we conclude with Sect. 6.

2   Related Work

In this section, we explore other work that focuses on generating smart contracts and blockchain applications based on higher-level specifications.

Minacori [8] has developed a web application allowing users to specify and deploy ERC-20 Tokens on the Ethereum blockchain [9]. ERC-20 Tokens are typically used to represent a cryptocurrency and are implemented by means of a smart contract. The tool allows the user to customize the token to their needs, by providing a number of purchase plans. Compared to our work, the scope of the smart contract generation is more limited as it only allows users to create tokens on the blockchain. In addition to generating contracts for each defined token, we also provide the user the ability to specify rules that should be executed automatically under certain conditions and to limit the types of transaction that may be executed in the use case.

Regnath and Steinhors propose "SmaCoNat", a natural language specification that allows to write smart contracts in a more human understandable form [10]. It provides a safer execution environment, as the expressiveness of existing smart contract languages could lead to dangerous system behavior - even if not intended by the programmer. To reach their goals, the authors restrict the freedom of the programmer to less complex programming constructs and a safer execution area. Although "SmaCoNat" is a language that seems to be less complex than existing smart contract languages, it does not seem to be focused on non-programmers, and still involves writing actual code from scratch with quite some programming constructs, as opposed to our framework.

The approach of Frantz and Nowostawski [11] is based on a grammar consisting of different components, including: "Attributes", "Deontic", "Aim", "Conditions" and "Or Else", known as ADICO. In chronological order, one has to specify the actors involved in the use case, the nature of the statement, the actions to be taken, the restrictions (if any), and the actions to perform in case of non-conformance with the given restrictions. Although the solution is focused on non-programmers, it seems that smart contract developers are still required during the contract generation process. Compared to our approach, this approach seems to be less intuitive since it still requires specifying pseudo-code. Also, the approach is not tailored to a specific domain as ours, meaning that constructs common to a particular domain need to be specified for each use case in that domain.

SPESC [12] uses another approach to generate smart contracts. The authors propose a custom specification language based on domain concepts such as parties, terms, conditions, and transactions. However, the language involves constructs as in existing programming languages, such as query-type languages and class-type languages, requiring the user to have basic programming skills, as opposed to our approach. TA-SPESC, an extended version of SPESC [13], is similar in this way.

In [14] smart contracts are generated based on requirements specified in a user interface using "Petri Nets". Petri Nets provide a graphical modeling technique that allows to visualize the logic of a workflow. It uses the concepts: places, transitions, and tokens. The Petri Nets approach looks interesting, but the paper does not report on a user evaluation. The current prototype seems to be targeting advanced users, as the use of Petri Nets for modeling seems rather complex and may require some training.

Allouche et al. present a generic blockchain-agnostic architectural framework that automatically produces and executes Smart Contracts from Internet Of Media Things (IoMT) information [15]. The framework requires a domain expert from the IoMT field and one from the blockchain field for each use case. The IoMT expert gives the specifications for the use case (based on the ISO/IEC 23093 standard) whereas the blockchain expert develops smart contract prototypes to be used within that use case. The information is combined and given to a "Smart Contract Developer" that generates the contracts. Although their goal is similar, the domain is different from ours; use cases are limited to IoMT devices. Also, a blockchain expert is required to facilitate the contract generation for each use case, as opposed to our work.

In [16], a framework for the auto-generation of smart contracts is presented using ontologies and semantic rules to represent the domain knowledge of the use case, and a smart contract template. While our framework is tailored towards resource exchange, this ontology approach can be used for a much broader range of applications. However, this means that first an ontology needs to be developed and the sematic rules need to be expressed in SWRL; two tasks that require time and technical expertise.

Lu et al. [17] introduce modeling methods to create models for assets and cross-organizational business processes, and methods to translate these models to smart contracts by generating smart contract code, based on a Model-Driven Engineering (MDE) approach. Also, they provide tools to deploy the generated contracts and to interact with them after deployment. The MDE approach allows users to specify requirements through models instead of writing smart contract code, so that well-tested code can be generated, avoiding crucial vulnerabilities. The associated tool Lorikeet is presented in [18]. It is useable for complex business processes as it seems to be quite powerful. However, the downside is that its expressiveness could be too technical for non-IT skilled people. Also, the tool requires user input in a form that is closely tied to the syntax of the Solidity programming language.

Regerator [19] is a framework for generating smart contracts in Solidity for Ethereum, which allows storing registries (lists of information recorded and managed by a trusted authority) on the blockchain, using a model-driven approach. The tool also generates user interfaces that allow interaction with the generated registries as well as APIs. The approach used is similar to Lorikeet, but the use cases are limited to registries.

Fournier and Skarbovksy present a model-driven approach to enrich smart contracts with the ability to add temporal logic (reasoning over time) [20]. Their approach is focused on time-sensitive applications but does not seem to be suitable for people without IT knowledge, and the environment seems to be restricted to private blockchains.

3 Framework

To allow business people with little to no IT-skills to easily set up blockchain applications involving smart contracts for the exchange of resources, we proposed in [5], a framework that allows organizations to provide the specifications for their use case and generates the corresponding blockchain application. Currently the framework has been implemented; its architecture is given in Fig. 1. Businesspeople specify organization-specific details and the requirements for their use case through an easy-to-use browser interface provided by the Use Case Specification module (see Fig. 1 – Layer 1). The name of the use case, the organizations involved in the use case, the persons authorized to send resources on behalf of the organizations (called "owners"), the users who may receive and consume resources (called "end users") (only needed if one wants to restrict the potential set of end users), the resource types involved (e.g., points, certificates), the allowed operation types (i.e., transactions) (e.g., awarding loyalty points to customers), and actions that should be executed automatically following one or more transactions (e.g., an action that compensates a company when a customer uses his loyalty points for a purchase with another company), need to be specified. For entering these specifications, an easy-to-use user interface has been developed and evaluated with potential users. This interface is described in [6]. The user evaluation was done by eight people having a business background, with the purpose of evaluating the usability of the interface for non-IT skilled people and obtaining feedback on the usefulness of the framework. Positive results and feedback were obtained.

After defining the specifications for the use case, all required smart contracts are generated automatically by the Smart Contract Generation Module (see Fig. 1 – Layer 2). After generation, these smart contracts can be deployed on a blockchain of choice (e.g., Ethereum [21], Polygon [22]). When using a public blockchain, the resulting resource-exchange application will guarantee true ownership of resources for end users. On private blockchains that are generally less decentralized, as they are typically ran by a much smaller number of nodes, the possibility to reduce the transaction costs is more likely but the same level of true ownership of resources is not guaranteed.

After a use case system is deployed to a blockchain, an application is provided by the Use Case Interaction module (see Fig. 1 – Layer 1), that allows the actual exchange of resources between the organizations and the end users of the use case.

This paper explains how, and which smart contracts are generated for a use case.

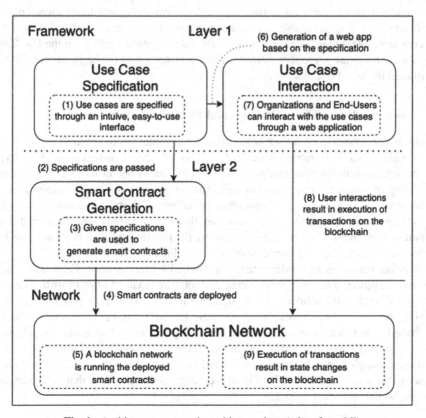

Fig. 1. Architecture, network, and interactions (taken from [6])

4   Generation of Smart Contracts

We first describe the mapping between the concepts used in the Use Case Specification module and smart contract concepts. On purpose, the Use Case Specification module does not use terminology or concepts from the domain of blockchain as we target people without knowledge of blockchain and smart contracts, but it uses concepts that are understandable by businesspeople (referred to as user concepts). It was confirmed by the user evaluation mentioned in Sect. 3 that these concepts are indeed understandable for business users. Next, we elaborate on how the specifications are translated into smart contracts. We use an example throughout the explanation: a "Loyalty Points" use case, having two grocery stores (A and B) as organizations, John as a customer and loyalty points as resource type. Both stores use the same type of loyalty points (meaning that a loyalty point has the same value in both stores). In the example, grocery store A awards 100 loyalty points to John for buying vegetables. Next, John uses these earned points in grocery store B to get a discount on the purchase of some fruits. For such cases, the grocery stores agreed upon an automatic financial settlement (defined in the Use Case Specification module): grocery store B should transfer a part of the points (i.e., 10%) consumed by John back to store A.

4.1   Mapping Between User Concepts and Blockchain Concepts

In blockchain systems, each user is identified by a wallet (as opposed to a traditional login) [23]. A wallet is used to hold digital resources (known as tokens, such as cryptocurrencies or non-fungible tokens (NFTs)), and contains one or more accounts, each consisting of a public and private key pair. The private key of a wallet is used to sign transactions (that typically involve sending/spending of digital resources), whilst the public key should be given to other users such that they are able to receive/earn digital resources from them. The wallet owner (having the private key) is in full control of his wallets' resources, meaning they cannot be manipulated by any other party.

Sending resources to another wallet, is handled by transactions. Each transaction consists of a sender, a receiver, the resource, and some metadata. A blockchain transaction is only valid when the sender digitally signs the transaction with its private key. After signing, the sender broadcasts the signed transaction. Then, the transaction is to be confirmed (either by a miner or a validator, depending on the exact setup of the blockchain [24, 25]), making the receiver the new owner of the resource.

In our mapping, wallets are used to identify each user (i.e., each end user and each owner of an organization) involved in the resource exchange. Note that users can use existing wallets if they have one.

Note that smart contracts are little "programs" running on a blockchain, that, once deployed, cannot be changed [26, 27]. They can change the state of the blockchain, such as ownership of resources, based on certain conditions. Such contracts can also hold resources (like wallets do) and release these according to programmed conditions.

As most smart contracts compilers set limitations on smart contract sizes, the logic for each use case needs to be spread across multiple smart contracts and libraries. A library is a special kind of smart contract that contains reusable code (such as functions and structures) but typically does not store any variables.

Since in our approach, transactions performed by the organizations can be initiated by multiple "owners" (see Sect. 3), the concept of organization is implemented as (mapped onto) a smart contract, allowing all defined owners (each identified by a wallet) to execute transactions on behalf of the organization. Also, having a smart contract for each organization allows to enforce rules, such as the financial settlements defined in the Use Case Specification module.

We consider two types of resources: Fungible Resource Types (FRT), which are typically used for cryptocurrencies, and Non-Fungible Resource Types (NRFT), which are used to represent something unique, such as an artwork or collectibles. In our approach, every resource type is implemented with a smart contract (a token contract) that is based on the "ERC Token standard" [28]. A token is an individual representation of ownership on the blockchain of a specific asset. A token contract controls the ownership of each of the individual tokens of a specific type.

The Use Case Specification module allows users to limit the operations that can take place in the use case by specifying allowed operation types. The logic for the operation types will be stored in a smart contract.

With the help of "if" and "then" constructs, organizations can specify rules (e.g., the settlement rules) indicating the (set of) operation(s) that should occur, based on a (set of) operations that have occurred. The logic to execute these rules, as well as the rules themselves, are stored in a smart contract. For example, in the "Loyalty Points" use case introduced above, the rule for the financial settlement is (informally): "IF store A awards X loyalty points to John AND John spends Y points ($Y \leq X$) in store B, THEN store B has to transfer $Y*10/100$ points (i.e., 10% of Y) to store A."

Table 1 provides an overview of the mapping of the user concepts used in Layer 1 to blockchain concepts used in Layer 2. The first column gives the name of the user concept, and the second column gives the concept on which it is mapped.

Table 1. Mapping of UI concepts from Layer 1 to Blockchain concepts

UI concept	→	Blockchain concept
End user	→	Wallet
Owner (of organization)	→	Wallet
Organization	→	Smart Contract
Resource type	→	Smart Contract
Resource	→	Token[a]
Operation type	→	Smart Contract
Operation	→	Transaction[a]
Rule	→	"Smart Contract Rule"[b]
Rules	→	Smart Contract

[a] Implemented as logic in a smart contract.
[b] Not a native blockchain concept; implemented as logic in a smart contract.

4.2 Generated Smart Contracts

The contracts in our current implementation are generated for Solidity[1], a smart contract language supported by many blockchains such as Ethereum [21] and Polygon [22]. Implementations for other smart contract languages (such as Rust[2]) can always be added, as the specifications are independent of the smart contract language used.

Figure 2 shows a high-level overview of the most relevant fields and methods of each contract generated. We describe the functionality of each type of contract and library generated below.

Token Contract. This contract keeps track of the ownership of each individual token involved and some generic properties of the token type, such as the common name of the tokens and the total token supply (in case of an ERC-20 token).

As pointed out in Sect. 4.1, tokens can be fungible (FT) or non-fungible (NFT). FTs are implemented by contracts based on the ERC-20 standard, and NFTs are implemented by contracts based on the ERC-721 standard. These standards include naming conventions, as well as the functionality that the contracts should have, such as the "transfer" function. Following these standards allows for compatibility with many other blockchain applications built with smart contracts, such as the transfer of tokens across apps (outside the current use case), contracts and wallets. Listing 1-3 shows example code of a fungible token contract (i.e., loyalty points) in the context of the "Loyalty Points" use case.

---

[1] https://docs.soliditylang.org/.
[2] https://www.rust-lang.org/.

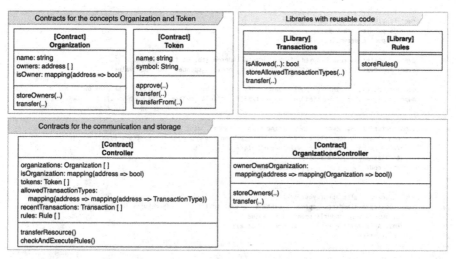

Fig. 2. High-level overview of most relevant fields & methods in generated smart contracts

```
1 ∨ abstract contract Token{
2       string  public name;
3       string  public symbol;
4
5 ∨     constructor(string memory _name, string memory _symbol){
6           name=_name;
7           symbol=_symbol;
8       }
9
10      function approve(address _spender, uint256 _value) public virtual returns (bool success);
11      function transfer(address _to, uint256 _value) public virtual returns (bool success);
12      function transferFrom(address _from, address _to, uint256 _value) public virtual returns (bool success);
13
14  }
```
Listing 1. Token contract for fungible and non-fungible tokens

OrganizationsController Contract. This contract keeps track of all organizations involved in the use case and is used as gateway to communicate to the contracts of each organization. This is the only contract that is allowed to initiate the transfer of resources outwards of an organization. This contract is illustrated in Listing 4.

Organization Contract. Each organization participating in the use case is represented by a contract on the blockchain. This contract keeps track of the individual properties of the organizations, such as a unique ID, and all its owners. Listing 5-6 shows an example of an Organization Contract (for store A) in the context of the "Loyalty Points" use case.

```
1   contract FungibleToken is Token{
2       uint256 public totalSupply;
3       uint8   public decimals = 18;
4
5       event Transfer(address indexed _from, address indexed _to, uint256 _value);
6       event Approval(address indexed _owner, address indexed _spender, uint256 _value);
7
8       mapping(address => uint256) public balanceOf; //(a -> b): number of tokens b held by owner a
9       mapping(address => mapping(address => uint256)) public allowance; //(a -> b -> c): a allows b
10                                                                       // to spend its c number of tokens
11
12      constructor(string memory _name, string memory _symbol, uint _totalSupply) Token(_name, _symbol){
13          //Initially assign all the tokens to the person who deployed the contract (msg.sender)
14          //The actual distribution will occur later
15          totalSupply = _totalSupply;
16          balanceOf[msg.sender] = _totalSupply;
17      }
18
19      //Lets someone else spent your tokens
20      function approve(address _spender, uint256 _value) public override returns (bool success) {
21          allowance[msg.sender][_spender] = _value;
22          emit Approval(msg.sender, _spender, _value);
23          return true;
24      }
25
26      //Sends token from this contract to an outside wallet
27      function transfer(address _to, uint256 _value) public override returns (bool success) {
28          require(balanceOf[msg.sender] >= _value);
29          balanceOf[msg.sender] -= _value;
30          balanceOf[_to] += _value;
31          emit Transfer(msg.sender, _to, _value);
32          return true;
33      }
34
35      //Sends tokens from an outside wallet to this contract
36      function transferFrom(address _from, address _to, uint256 _value) public override returns (bool success) {
37          require(_value <= balanceOf[_from]);
38          require(_value <= allowance[_from][msg.sender]);
39          balanceOf[_from] -= _value;
40          balanceOf[_to] += _value;
41          allowance[_from][msg.sender] -= _value;
42          //emit Transfer(_from, _to, _value);
43          return true;
44      }
45  }
```

Listing 2. Token contract for fungible tokens

```
1 v contract LoyaltyPoints is FungibleToken{
2
3 v    constructor(string memory _name, string memory _symbol, uint _totalSupply)
4          FungibleToken(_name, _symbol, _totalSupply){
5          //Specific properties here (if any)
6      }
7 }
```

Listing 3. Example code of generated smart contract for a fungible token

Transactions Library. This library contains logic that is required to model and execute transactions on the blockchain, and to check whether the execution of a transaction should be allowed or rejected (according to the specifications given). A "transaction" is an actual transfer of one or more tokens on the blockchain, consisting of exactly one sender, one receiver, a token and a token amount (e.g., Alice sends 3 Ethereum to Bob) [2]. We use "transaction types" to define the transactions that are allowed to be executed in the use case system. The "transfer" function allows to execute an actual transfer. If a transaction does not match a defined transaction type, the transaction is not allowed, and it will revert. Otherwise, and if the sender owns the token(s) requested to transfer, the transaction is executed.

```
1   contract OrganizationsController{
2
3       Controller controller;
4
5       struct OwnerOrganization{
6           Organization organization;
7           address owner;
8       }
9
10      //Does the given owner own the given organization?
11      mapping(address => mapping(Organization => bool)) public ownerOwnsOrganization;
12                                              //(owner, Organization) -> isOwnerOf
13
14      constructor(OwnerOrganization [] memory ownerOfOrganization, Controller _controller ) {
15          controller = _controller;
16          for(uint i=0; i<ownerOfOrganization.length;i++){
17              ownerOwnsOrganization[ownerOfOrganization[i].owner][ownerOfOrganization[i].organization] = true;
18          }
19      }
20
21      //Public Transfer Function: Owners of an organization can call this
22      //function (through controller contract), to transfer tokens to customers
23      function transfer(Token _token, address _org, address _dest, uint _amount) public returns(bool){
24          require(msg.sender == address(controller), "Only controller contract can call this function!");
25          //If the sender is on the owner list of the given organization (checked by Controller)
26          //, transfer "_amount" of tokens in the name of the organization.
27          return Organization(_org).transfer(_token, _dest, _amount);
28      }
29  }
```
Listing 4. Smart contract code of OrganizationsController

```
1   abstract contract Organization {
2
3       //Transfer tokens from organization to destination
4       function transfer(Token token, address _dest, uint _amount) public virtual returns(bool);
5   }
```
Listing 5. Contract for an organization

Rules Library. Rules are used to express transactions that should be executed automatically based on a set of conditions. As indicated, a rule contains a series of IF and THEN statements. Each IF statement consists of one or more senders, receivers, a token with a corresponding amount range, which describes a (range of) transaction(s).

Everything needed to model and store rules (including enums, structs and mappings) is stored in this library. The function "storeRules" stores the given rules on the blockchain, to facilitate the actual execution of rules when required.

Controller Contract. This contract acts as the main controller of all contracts. It is responsible for executing all user interactions (i.e., transfer of resources) in the use case[3]. In addition to facilitating transfers, this contract also stores all token types involved, the

---

[3] Note that transactions between end users outside the use case system are always possible (since any wallet software facilitates this) and thus do not require interaction with any of the above specified contracts. This ensures that end users possess true ownership of their resources.

allowed transaction types, and rules. The function "checkAndExecuteRules" verifies whether any specified rules should be executed using the following algorithm. Whenever a transaction is executed, the last IF statement of each rule is compared to that transaction. In case that the transaction matches this statement, and the rule contains multiple IF statements, another recent transaction is sought that matches the IF statement preceding this IF statement in the rule. If such transaction is found, this process continues until no IF statements are left. If a match is found for each of the IF statements in the rule, all transactions in the THEN part of the rule are executed, and the algorithm terminates. If, during this process, no match is found, the algorithm restarts by looking for matches for the next rule. The algorithm is given in pseudo-code in Listing 7.

```
1   contract StoreA9902 is Organization{
2
3       address owner; //Deployer of the contract
4
5       //Used Contracts
6       OrganizationsController middleware; //middleware used to interact with this contract
7       bool middlewareSet = false;
8
9       //Organization Details
10      string public uuid = "5910ec25-ecb2-4526-9c97-bfdf84a09902";
11      string public name = "Store A";
12      string public identifier = "store-a-9902";
13      string public vat_nr = "123.456.789"
14      string public address = "";
15
16      //Owners of organization
17      address[] public owners;
18      mapping(address => bool) public isOwner;
19                              .
20      constructor(string memory _name, address[] memory _owners){
21          name = _name;
22          owner = msg.sender; //Store the owner (deployer of the contract)
23
24          owners = _owners; //Set the Owners of the Organization
25          for(uint i=0; i<_owners.length;i++)
26              isOwner[_owners[i]] = true;
27      }
28
29      function setMiddleware(OrganizationsController _middleware) onlyOwner public{
30          require(!middlewareSet, "Middleware can only be set once, by the owner of the contract");
31          middleware = _middleware;
32          middlewareSet = true;
33      }
34
35      //Public Transfer Function
36      function transfer(Token _token, address _dest, uint _amount) setupDone override public returns(bool){
37          require(msg.sender == address(middleware), "Only the middleware contract can interact with this contract");
38          return _token.transfer(_dest, _amount);
39      }
40
41      modifier onlyOwner(){
42          require(msg.sender == owner, "The sender calling this function must be the owner of the contract"); _;
43      }
44
45      modifier setupDone(){
46          require(middlewareSet, "The middleware contract must be set before interacting with this contract"); _;
47      }
48  }
```

Listing 6. Example code of generated smart contract for an organization

4.3 Examples

In this section we give some examples on how the resources can be exchanged.

Transfer of Resources from an Organization to an End User. Figure 4 illustrates the scenario in which organization A has one owner "Mark" who initiates a transfer of a number of tokens of type 1 to end user John (a customer). To transfer resources for organization A, a call of the "transfer" function of the Controller is needed, which checks whether Mark (the sender) is indeed in the list of owners of organization A (through the OrganizationsController Contract) and then calls the "transfer" function of the "Transaction" Contract. This function will check whether the proposed transaction matches the "allowedTransactionTypes" and will then call the "transfer" function of the Organizations Controller Contract, which calls the "transfer" function of the contract of the organization that transfers resources (in this case organization A). Then, the contract of organization A calls the "transfer" function of the Transactions Contract. This function will check whether the proposed transaction matches the "allowedTransactionTypes" and will call the "transfer" function of the token contract. If all checks pass, an actual transfer of the tokens of type 1 to the wallet of John (the receiver) takes place. After the transfer, the Controller Contract checks whether any rules should be executed through the mechanism explained in Sect. 4.2.

```
1   define LT as the last executed transaction
2   add LT to {recent transactions}
3 ▾ for Rule Ri in {all defined rules} do: ruleLoop
4       define LFi as last IFStatement of Ri
5 ▾     if Transaction LT matches IFStatement LFi then
6           #last transaction LT matches last IFStatement LFi
7           define FSi as {all IFStatements of Ri except LFi}
8           define RFSi as reversed order of FSi
9 ▾         for IFStatement Fi in RFSi do
10              define RT as {all recent transactions except LT}
11              define MT as NULL
12 ▾            for Transaction Tj in RT do
13 ▾                if Transaction Tj matches IFStatement Fi:
14                      #found matching transaction Tj for IFStatement Fi
15                      MT = Tj
16                      break
17                  endif
18              endfor
19 ▾            if MT is null
20                  #no matching transaction found for IFStatement Fi for Ri
21                  #go to next rule (next iteration of rule loop)
22                  continue ruleLoop
23              endif
24          #found matching transaction for each IFStatement
25          #execute all then statements of Rule Ri
26 ▾        for ThenStatement Ti in Ri:
27              execute THENStatement Ti
28          endfor
29          return 'all rules from Ri executed'
30 ▾    else
31          #no matching transaction found for the last IFStatement LFi
32          return 'no rules executed'
33      endif
34  endfor
35
36  #no rules defined
37  return 'no rules executed'
```

Listing 7. Pseudo code for the "checkAndExecuteRules" function of the Controller Contract.

Internal Transfers. Transfers between organizations occur in the same way as in the example above, except that instead of an end user an Organization Contract is used.

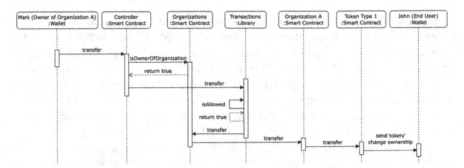

Fig. 4. Example scenario of transfer of tokens from an Organization to an End User

Transfer from an End User to an Organization. Figure 5 illustrates the scenario in which an end user transfers resources to an organization. Here, an end user John initiates the transfer of a number of tokens of type 1 to organization A, by calling (through the Use Case Interaction module) the "transfer" function of the Controller Contract, which calls the "transfer" function of the "Transaction" Contract. This function will check whether the proposed transaction matches the "allowedTransactionTypes" and will call the "transfer" function of the token contract for token 1, that transfers the tokens of type 1 to organization A (the receiver). After the transfer, the Controller Contract checks whether any rules should be executed through the mechanism explained in Sect. 4.2.

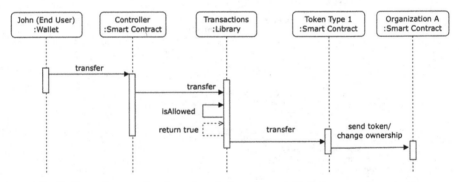

Fig. 5. Example scenario of transfer of tokens from an End User to an Organization

5 Discussion and Limitations

Currently only the generation of smart contracts for Solidity is supported. Although this is one of the most popular smart contract languages that can be used by a wide variety of blockchain networks [29], also generating contracts in other languages would give more flexibility. Note that implementations for other languages can be added.

For any system that generates software, it is important to guarantee in some way that the generated software satisfies the specifications. In our case, the allowed transactions and the specified rules should be executed correctly. Currently, we verified this by writing tests for one particular use case. All tests passed successfully. In future work we will investigate how we can generate tests automatically for different use cases.

Nowadays systems need to be flexible. For instance, it would be desirable to allow new organizations to join an existing resource-exchange platform. In that case, it may also be necessary to review certain rules and settlements. Ideally such changes should not affect the working of the already deployed application. At the moment, this is not implemented yet. This is the subject of future work.

Although the contracts were developed with efficiency in mind, still some work can be done to make the contracts more resource-efficient, resulting in faster execution of transactions and less gas fees (means of payment for transactions). Of course, this also greatly depends on the type of blockchain running the contracts.

For now, the involved transaction fees for deploying the generated contracts, and interacting with the contracts after deployment, need to be covered by the initiator of the transaction. In some cases, it might be desired that some organizations (participating in the use case) should be accountable for such costs. How to realize this without compromising the main principles of the system (decentralization and full ownership of resources) requires further investigation.

6 Conclusion

In this paper, we discussed the automatic generation of the smart contracts needed to perform transfers of resources in the context of resource exchange platforms for which the specifications for a use case are given by means of high-level information by non-IT skilled people. Also, logic is generated to check and execute specified rules, e.g., to accomplish financial settlements between organizations. Several smart contracts and libraries are generated for a use case. Currently, the smart contracts are generated for Solidity, which runs on many popular blockchains. However, the generation process can be extended to support other languages and platforms as well.

We explained the mapping from the high-level user concepts used in the Use Case Specification module to specify a use case and tailored towards non-IT skilled people, onto the technical concepts used in blockchain technology. We also explained the different types of contracts generated and their role and functionality. The exchange of resources by means of these smart contracts is illustrated with some examples.

As part of future research work, we will investigate if and how the framework could generate tests for the generated smart contracts of a use case and how to allow to make changes to a deployed use case application. Furthermore, we plan to further finetune the generation process to generate blockchain applications that are more cost-efficient and to allow to have transactions paid by parties other than the initiator.

References

1. Scherer, M.: Performance and scalability of blockchain networks and smart contracts (2017)
2. Underwood, S.: Blockchain beyond bitcoin. Commun. ACM. **59**, 15–17 (2016). https://doi. org/10.1145/2994581
3. Chauhan, A., Malviya, O.P., Verma, M., Mor, T.S.: Blockchain and scalability. In: Proceedings of 2018 IEEE 18th International Conference on Software Quality, Reliability and Security, QRS-C 2018. 122–128 (2018). https://doi.org/10.1109/QRS-C.2018.00034.
4. Parizi, R.M., Dehghantanha, A.: Smart contract programming languages on blockchains: an empirical evaluation of usability and security. In: Chen, S., Wang, H., Zhang, L.J. (eds.) ICBC 2018. LNCS, vol. 10974, pp. 75–91. Springer, Cham (2018). https://doi.org/10.1007/978-3-319-94478-4_6
5. Soni, K.: A trustable platform for exchange of resources across organizations and their customers. In: Middleware 2019 - Proceedings of the 2019 20th International Middleware Conference Doctoral Symposium, Part of Middleware 2019, pp. 20–22. Association for Computing Machinery, Inc. (2019). https://doi.org/10.1145/3366624.3368160
6. Soni, K., De Troyer, O.: Specifying blockchain-based resource-exchange systems by business-level users using a generic easy-to-use framework. In: Arai, K. (eds.) Proceedings of the Future Technologies Conference (FTC) 2022, Volume 2. LNNS, vol 560, Springer, Cham (2023). https://doi.org/10.1007/978-3-031-18458-1_3
7. Soni, K., De Troyer, O.: Generating smart contracts for blockchain-based resource-exchange systems. In: Pardede, E., Delir Haghighi, P., Khalil, I., Kotsis, G. (eds.) Information Integration and Web Intelligence, iiWAS 2022. LNCS, vol 13635, Springer, Cham (2022). https://doi. org/10.1007/978-3-031-21047-1_9
8. ERC20 Token Generator | Create ERC20 Token for FREE. https://vittominacori.github.io/ erc20-generator/. Accessed 05 Aug 2021
9. Buterin, V.: Ethereum: a next-generation smart contract and decentralized application platform (2014)
10. Regnath, E., Steinhorst, S.: SmaCoNat: smart contracts in natural language. In: 2018 Forum on Specification & Design Languages (FDL) (2018). https://doi.org/10.1109/FDL.2018.852 4068.
11. Frantz, C.K., Nowostawski, M.: From institutions to code: towards automated generation of smart contracts. In: Proceedings - IEEE 1st International Workshops on Foundations Applications of Self-Systems, FAS-W 2016, pp. 210–215 (2016). https://doi.org/10.1109/FAS-W. 2016.53.
12. He, X., Qin, B., Zhu, Y., Chen, X., Liu, Y.: SPESC: a specification language for smart contracts. In: Proceedings - International Computing Software Application Conference, vol. 1, pp. 132–137 (2018). https://doi.org/10.1109/COMPSAC.2018.00025.
13. Zhu, Y., Song, W., Wang, D., Ma, D., Chu, W.C.C.: TA-SPESC: toward asset-driven smart contract language supporting ownership transaction and rule-based generation on blockchain. IEEE Trans. Reliab. **70**, 1255–1270 (2021). https://doi.org/10.1109/TR.2021.3054617
14. Zupan, N., Kasinathan, P., Cuellar, J., Sauer, M.: Secure smart contract generation based on petri nets. In: Rosa Righi, Rodrigo da, Alberti, Antonio Marcos, Singh, Madhusudan (eds.) Blockchain Technology for Industry 4.0. BT, pp. 73–98. Springer, Singapore (2020). https:// doi.org/10.1007/978-981-15-1137-0_4
15. Allouche, M., Mitrea, M., Moreaux, A., Kim, S.K.: Automatic smart contract generation for internet of media things. ICT Express. **7**, 274–277 (2021). https://doi.org/10.1016/J.ICTE. 2021.08.009
16. Choudhury, O., Rudolph, N., Sylla, I., Fairoza, N., Das, A.: Auto-generation of smart contracts from domain-specific ontologies and semantic rules. In: Proceedings - IEEE 2018

International Congress Cybermatics 2018 IEEE Conference on Internet Things, Green Computing Communication Cyber, Physical Society Computing Smart Data, Blockchain, Computing Information Technology iThings/Gree, pp. 963–970 (2018). https://doi.org/10.1109/CYBERMATICS_2018.2018.00183.

17. Lu, Q., et al.: Integrated model-driven engineering of blockchain applications for business processes and asset management. Softw. Pract. Exp. **51**, 1059–1079 (2021). https://doi.org/10.1002/SPE.2931

18. Tran, A.B., Lu, Q., Weber, I.: Lorikeet: a model-driven engineering tool for blockchain-based business process execution and asset management. In: 16th International Conference on Business Process Management, Sydney, Australia, p. 5 (2018)

19. Tran, A.B., Xu, S., Weber, I., Staples, M., Rimba, P.: Regerator: a registry generator for blockchain. In: 29th International Conference on Advanced Information Systems Engineering (CaiSE2017), Essen, Germany, pp. 81–88 (2017).

20. Fournier, F., Skarbovsky, I.: Enriching smart contracts with temporal aspects. In: Joshi, J., Nepal, S., Zhang, Q., Zhang, L.-J. (eds.) ICBC 2019. LNCS, vol. 11521, pp. 126–141. Springer, Cham (2019). https://doi.org/10.1007/978-3-030-23404-1_9

21. Home I ethereum.org. https://ethereum.org/en/. Accessed 02 June 2022

22. Polygon. https://polygon.technology/. Accessed 04 June 2022

23. Mahmoud, Q.H., Lescisin, M., AlTaei, M.: Research challenges and opportunities in blockchain and cryptocurrencies. Internet Technol. Lett. **2**, e93 (2019). https://doi.org/10.1002/ITL2.93

24. Nguyen, G.T., Kim, K.: A survey about consensus algorithms used in blockchain. J. Inf. Process. Syst. **14**, 101–128 (2018). https://doi.org/10.3745/JIPS.01.0024

25. Sorensen, D.: Establishing standards for consensus on blockchains. In: Joshi, J., Nepal, S., Zhang, Q., Zhang, LJ. (eds.) ICBC 2019. LNCS, vol. 11521, pp. 18–33. Springer, Cham (2019). https://doi.org/10.1007/978-3-030-23404-1_2/FIGURES/3

26. Christidis, K., Devetsikiotis, M.: Blockchains and smart contracts for the internet of things. IEEE Access. **4**, 2292–2303 (2016). https://doi.org/10.1109/ACCESS.2016.2566339

27. Giancaspro, M.: Is a 'smart contract' really a smart idea? Insights from a legal perspective. Comput. Law Secur. Rev. **33**, 825–835 (2017). https://doi.org/10.1016/J.CLSR.2017.05.007

28. ERC I Ethereum Improvement Proposals. https://eips.ethereum.org/erc. Accessed 09 Mar 2022

29. Macdonald, M., Liu-Thorrold, L., Julien, R.: The blockchain: a comparison of platforms and their uses beyond bitcoin (2017). https://doi.org/10.13140/RG.2.2.23274.52164

A Community Detection-Based Blockchain Sharding Scheme

Zixu Zhang[1]([✉]), Xu Wang[1], Guangsheng Yu[2], Wei Ni[2], Ren Ping Liu[1],
Nektarios Georgalas[3], and Andrew Reeves[3]

[1] GBDTC, University of Technology Sydney, Sydney, Australia
`zixu.zhang@student.uts.edu.au`, {`xu.wang-1,renping.liu`}`@uts.edu.au`
[2] Data61, CSIRO, Sydney, Australia
{`saber.yu,wei.ni`}`@data61.csiro.au`
[3] Applied Research, British Telecom, Martlesham, UK
{`nektarios.georgalas,andrew.reeves`}`@bt.com`

Abstract. Sharding has been considered a promising approach to improving blockchain scalability. However, multiple shards result in a large number of cross-shard transactions, which require a long confirmation time across shards and thus restrain the scalability of sharded blockchains. In this paper, we convert the blockchain sharding challenge into a graph partitioning problem on undirected and weighted transaction graphs that capture transaction frequency between blockchain addresses. We propose a new sharding scheme using the community detection algorithm, where blockchain nodes in the same community frequently trade with each other. The detected communities are used as shards for node allocation. The proposed community detection-based sharding scheme is validated using public Ethereum transactions over one million blocks. The proposed community detection-based sharding scheme is able to reduce the ratio of cross-shard transactions from 80% to 20%, as compared to baseline random sharding schemes, and retain the ratio of around 20% over the examined one million blocks.

Keywords: Blockchain · Sharding · Community detection

1 Introduction

Scalability is one of the well-known bottlenecks in the development of blockchain technology. The scalability of a blockchain refers to its ability to process more transactions per unit of time. Many blockchain platforms, such as Bitcoin [1] and Ethereum (ETH) [2] (about seven transactions per second for Bitcoin and about fifteen for Ethereum), are inefficient in processing transactions per unit of time. The scalability of blockchain has become increasingly important as blockchain is being used in different scenarios [3–5]. Blockchain platforms process transactions much slower than VISA, which processes 56,000 transactions per second [6].

Supported by BT Group Plc.

The scalability of blockchain has been studied extensively to increase transaction rates [7,8]. Shading technology is the most potential technology to improve blockchain scalability among many scaling schemes. For blockchains to become scalable, various sharding solutions have been introduced in [9–13].

Sharding is implemented on-chain, making it part of the layer-1 scaling solution [7]. Scaling on layer 1 has two directions, vertical scaling and horizontal scaling [14,15]. Vertical scaling of a chain involves increasing the transaction capacity within each block or shortening the block period. Vertical scaling increases transaction throughput, but it requires more bandwidth from nodes. As a result, vertical scaling methods are not feasible for nodes with limited bandwidth. Sharding is a horizontal scaling scheme that divides the blockchain into multiple parts. Each independent chain only responds to its transaction mining. As the number of shards increases, transaction throughput increases linearly [16].

Blockchain sharding increases transaction throughput, but cross-shard transactions also increase during sharding. Due to excessive cross-shard transactions, the sharding technique cannot scale efficiently in the blockchain [17,18]. Transactions between senders and recipients on different shards are termed cross-shard transactions, while intra-shard transactions are transactions within the same shard. Cross-shard transactions require multi-phase protocols to verify their authenticity. A multi-phase protocol typically consists of a prepare and a commit phase [19]. Since cross-shard transactions take longer to process and require more processing power than intra-shard transactions, sharding in the blockchain is not as effective in improving scalability when cross-shard transactions are involved. In [10], more than 95% of transactions are cross-shard transactions. Thus, reducing cross-shard transactions with efficient shard allocation strategies is a direct way to optimize sharding.

This paper intends to reduce the transactions between shards by allocating frequent blockchain node pairs to the same shard. We transform the problem of obtaining the least number of cross-shard transactions into a graph partition problem. A weighted and undirected graph is constructed using the number of transactions between nodes. Then, we propose generating the community result for assigning nodes to shards using a community detection algorithm. We demonstrate our scheme by testing its reliability and determining that cross-shard transactions are reduced to 20%. The following is a summary of our contributions.

- We convert the blockchain sharding challenge into a graph partitioning problem. The sharding optimization can be transformed into the community detection problem, where nodes are tightly linked with nodes in the same community and loosely connected with nodes in other communities.
- We propose a new sharding scheme using community-detection algorithms. The scheme is achieved by designing an undirected and weighted graph to

capture transactions where the weight of an edge represents the number of transactions between the endpoints. The graph is then divided into communities by running the community-detection algorithm, and each community forms a shard.

- Validated by comprehensive experiments on Ethereum transaction data, the proposed sharding scheme can significantly reduce the number of cross-shard transactions, e.g., from 80% to 20%, compared with popular random sharding schemes. Experiment results also confirm the stability of the proposed sharding scheme.

This paper is organized as follows. Section 2 introduces related blockchain sharding works. Section 3 depicts the proposed community detection-based sharding scheme. The experiment results are presented in Sect. 4, followed by conclusions in Sect. 5.

2   Related Work

Assigning nodes to shards is commonly accomplished by adding Distributed Randomness Generation (DRG) protocols to enhance the randomness of the assignment process. Elastico [9], Omniledger [10], and RapidChain [11] all use DRG protocols to randomly allocate nodes to shards. In [9], nodes are assigned to a shard according to the last few bits of the solution of the Proof of Work (PoW) puzzle. The PoW puzzle is derived from the combination of the epoch randomness, which is generated with a DRG protocol [20], node identity, and nonce.

Kokoris et al. [10] develope Omniledger, a distributed ledger where validators are randomly assigned to shards and synchronize the previous shard state. Each shard has a leader who is elected by a verified random function. The leader generates a randomness output for deriving a random permutation with other nodes by initiating the *RandHound* DRG [21] protocol. In subsequent allocations, no more than $\frac{1}{3}$ nodes at the beginning of the permutation are shuffled randomly to other shards. As with [9,10], Zamani et al. [11] propose a sharding-based blockchain protocol RapidChain. RapidChain uses different random allocation methods for nodes. In [11], the *reference committee* (a special shard) uses the Feldman Verifiable Secret Sharing (VSS) DRG [22] protocol to generate unbiased random outputs. The PoW puzzles are generated by random outputs and need to be solved by the nodes to join the system. Each node is then randomly assigned to each shard by a member of the *reference committee* executing *Commensal Cuckoo* rule [23]. With the *Commensal Cuckoo*, each node is mapped in a random position of Interval $[0, 1)$ based on its identity by a hash function. Interval $[0, 1)$ are then divided into regions representing shards. As new nodes are added, existing nodes in the same region are moved to new random regions.

Without a DRG protocol, node allocation to shards can also be achieved according to addresses' prefixes, such as Monoxide [12]. In addition to allocating nodes to shards based on addresses, nodes can be divided by voting from other nodes. For instance, Chainspace [13] permits nodes to move between shards based on the votes of other nodes. Through a smart contract called Manage-Shards, voting is carried out. By deploying different shards on different channels, Fabric [24,25] address sharding can be achieved. A trusted entity is used for cross-shard transactions.

Nodes can be assigned to shards using effective partitioning methods for reducing cross-shard transactions. Classical graph partitioning algorithms like Kernighan-Lin [26] can be used to optimize the sharding process. The Kernighan-Lin algorithm divides a graph into two communities of known size and exchanges any two vertices between them to obtain two communities with the smallest cut set size. The Kernighan-Lin algorithm causes multiple partitions since it divides two communities at once. Nevertheless, a multi-partitioned system will increase algorithm complexity.

Existing blockchain sharding schemes, including random sharding, voting-based sharding, and channel-based sharding, have not tried to improve the scalability of sharded blockchains by reducing the number of cross-shard transactions. Graph partitioning and community detection algorithms are promising to reduce cross-shard transactions but have yet to be developed for blockchain sharding schemes, especially for blockchains craving high scalability.

3   Proposed Community Detection-Based Sharding Scheme

We propose a novel blockchain sharding scheme using the community detection algorithm. An adjacency matrix representing transactions (TXs) between node pairs is used as the input parameter for the system model we presented. Our model uses the Louvain algorithm in community detection [27] to obtain communities that respond to the sharding result. All nodes are assumed to be trustworthy in the model. Under our assumption, cross-shard transactions are reduced to a lower frequency based on our model. Therefore, our community detection-based sharding model is more suitable for permissioned chains since security issue is out of scope. Notations used in this paper are collected in Table 1.

The blockchain sharding network is reviewed as an undirected weighted graph $G = (V, E)$. The set of vertices V represents node addresses, and the set of edge E represents the transaction number between node pairs. This G is incorporated into the community detection algorithm using the adjacency matrix format.

Figure 1 illustrates the sharding system we use to reduce R_c. This system performs four stages: Graph generation, Community detection, Community-based sharding, and Chain extension. The following Eq. 1 calculates the ratio of cross-shard transactions.

$$R_c = \frac{\phi_c}{\phi_i + \phi_c}. \tag{1}$$

Algorithm 1: Community-based sharding

▷ *Sharding($\mathcal{B}_p$, s)*

Input:
    $\mathcal{B}_p$: An epoch of blocks;
    s: The number of shards.

Output:
    $\mathcal{S}$: Shards with nodes;
    r: The cut weight ratio.

1   $\mathcal{A} = 0$
2   $\mathcal{N} \leftarrow$ **GetAllNodes**($\mathcal{B}_p$)
    `// Sort nodes according to the number of transactions.`
3   $\mathcal{N}_s \leftarrow$ **Sort**($\mathcal{N}$, TX)
4   **for** $i \le |\mathcal{N}_s|$ **do**
5   **for** $j \le |\mathcal{N}_s|$ **do**
7        $a_{i,j} \leftarrow$ **CountTX**($\mathcal{B}_p$, N_i, N_j)

8   $\mathcal{C} \leftarrow$ **CommunityDetection**($\mathcal{A}$, s)
    `// Calculate the cut weight ratio, which is the sum of weights of the edges crossing`
    `the communities divided by the sum of weights of all edges.`
9   $r \leftarrow$ **CalculateCutRatio**($\mathcal{A}$, $\mathcal{C}$)
10   $\mathcal{S} \leftarrow$ **MapNodesToCommunities**($\mathcal{N}_s$, $\mathcal{C}$)
11   **return** $\mathcal{S}, r$

▷ *ShardsExtension()*

Input:
    ρ: The threshold of cross-shard TX ratio;
    s: The number of shards.

12   **while** *True* **do**
13   **ShardsBlockMining()**
14   **if** *Shard heights reach an epoch* **then**
15       $\mathcal{B}_p \leftarrow$ **Blocks in the latest period**
16       $\phi_i \leftarrow$ **CountIntraShardTX**($\mathcal{B}_p$)
17       $\phi_c \leftarrow$ **CountCrossShardTX**($\mathcal{B}_p$)
18   **if** $\frac{\phi_c}{\phi_i + \phi_c} > \rho$ **then**
19         $\mathcal{S}, r =$ **Sharding**($\mathcal{B}_p$, s)
        `// Reallocated nodes to new shards.`
20   **ReAllocateNodes**($\mathcal{S}$)
21         $\rho \leftarrow$ max(ρ, r)

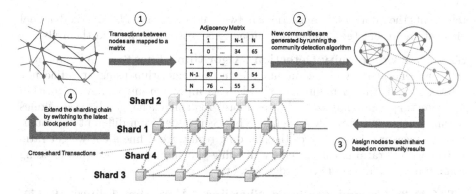

Fig. 1. The flow diagram of the proposed Re-sharding system comprising the following four stages. ① Graph generation: generate an adjacency matrix according to the number of transactions between nodes. ② Community detection: run the community detection algorithm to identify node communities so that nodes frequently exchange with nodes in the same community and less transact with nodes in different communities. ③ Community-based sharding: allocate nodes to shards according to detected communities, where nodes in the same community are in the same shard, and implement the sharding result. ④ Chain extension: extend the chains in parallel.

Table 1. notation and definition in the blockchain sharding system.

Notation	Description
$\mathcal{N}$	Set of nodes
$\mathcal{C}$	Set of community
$\mathcal{S}$	Set of shard
$\mathcal{B}_p$	An epoch of blocks
$\mathcal{E}_t$	t-th block epoch
r	The cut weight ratio
$\mathcal{A}$	The adjacency matrix of the transaction graph
s	The number of shards
ϕ_i	The number of Intra-shard transactions
ϕ_c	The number of Cross-shard transactions
ρ	Threshold for the cross-shard transaction ratio

STAGE 1: Graph Generation (Algorithm 1 lines 1–7). The model generates an adjacency matrix $\mathcal{A}$ based on the number of transactions between nodes. As shown in Algorithm 1, the adjacency matrix is initialized with zero. The algorithmic flow starts with obtaining the dataset of the node $\mathcal{N}$ that sends and receives transactions from the selected block epoch. Then, node dataset $\mathcal{N}$ are sorted based on the number of transactions to a sorted node dataset $\mathcal{N}_s$. An adjacency matrix $\mathcal{A}$ is generated after traversing all node sets. The size of the $\mathcal{A}$ depends on the node number. The i-th row and the j-th column in matrix $a_{i,j}$

represents the number of transactions between nodes N_i and N_j. Matrix diagonal elements represent the number of transactions between nodes and themselves.

STAGE 2: Community Detection (Algorithm 1 lines 8–9). A community set C is generated by the community detection algorithm using an adjacency matrix A and a fixed number of shards s as input parameters. An algorithm for detecting communities facilitates more frequent exchanges between nodes within a community and less exchange between nodes from different communities. To measure the quality of the sharding result, we define a cut weight ratio r. Cut weight ratio is calculated by dividing the sum of edge weights crossing communities by the sum of all edge weights.

STAGE 3: Community-based Sharding (Algorithm 1 lines 10–11). Based on the optimized outputs of the community set C from previous stages, sorted nodes are assigned to the new communities and the filled shard set S is returned. Filled shards set S with sorted nodes and a cut weight ratio r are returned at the end of each epoch.

STAGE 4: Chain Extension (Algorithm 1 lines 12–21). As the new shards returns, each chain mines blocks and extends in parallel until it reaches the end of an epoch. According to returned sharding results, the number of intra-chain transactions ϕ_i and the number of cross-chain transactions ϕ_c are separately counted. According to Eq. 1, the statistical results of both transactions are used to calculate a ratio of cross-shard transactions R_c. We set a threshold ρ for cross-shard transactions in our system. The threshold determines whether or not a node needs to be reassigned during a block epoch $\mathcal{E}_t$. A node is not re-allocated if R_c is less than the threshold. Otherwise, nodes are re-allocated to other shards based on the community detection algorithm. Additionally, the value of ρ is based on the largest R_c.

4   Experiments

4.1   Experiment Settings

An experimental framework is implemented in a local environment (MacBook Pro with 2.5 GHz Quad-Core Intel Core i7 and 16 GB memory) to evaluate a proposed blockchain sharding scheme. We create a virtual machine using Conda on Visual Studio Code and implement our framework in Python 3.10.44. Ethereum block data ranging from 13.7 million to 15.04 million are downloaded and sorted from the Ethereum public endpoint [28]. There are 1.34 million blocks in the captured block range. Experiments are conducted on consecutive 100,000 blocks randomly selected from captured block ranges. Our randomly selected block period is between 14 million and 14.9 million. We divide the selected block period into ten equal parts, each containing 10,000 blocks.

4.2   Data Overview

We have 762,203 node addresses and 3,735,641 transactions during our first test block epoch. The community detection algorithm uses the top 90 addresses[1] sending the most transaction numbers out of 762,203 addresses. We define K as the number of addresses with the most transactions in subsequent tests. After sorting the first 90 nodes, we see that the address with the most transactions belongs to OpenSea[2] In our first tested 10,000 blocks, OpenSea generates 154,879 transactions. Besides OpenSea, big companies like Coinbase[3] and Uniswap[4] also have large numbers of transactions on Ethereum. According to the adjacency matrix, 31 nodes do not have any transactions with any of the first 90 nodes. The row sum of all the 31 sender addresses in the matrix is zero. Thus we remove these 31 addresses, and the top 90 most transacted addresses form a 59×59 adjacency matrix.

4.3   Sharding Analysis

The comparison between a community detection-based sharding method and a random sharding method is shown in Fig. 2. In Fig. 2(a), the vertical axis represents the number of cross-shard transactions, while the horizontal axis represents the Ethereum block sequence number. Figure 2(b) differs from Fig. 2(a) in that the vertical axis represents the ratio of cross-shard transactions, while the horizontal axis remains the same. During the first block epoch, we divide the 59 addresses into four shards, which generate 76,369 transactions. As a result of adopting the community detection algorithm, 65,703 transactions are intra-shard transactions, and 10,666 are cross-shard transactions.

To compare with the community detection-based sharding scheme, we simulate a process of randomly assigning addresses, similar to the process of nodes randomly assigned to varying shards in Omniledger [10]. Nodes can be randomly allocated into shards of the same size. Alternatively, nodes can be randomly divided into shards of different sizes. Therefore, we develop two methods for randomly allocating nodes to shards in the experiments. Keeping each shard with the same number of nodes is balanced sharding. Sharding with more or fewer nodes in each shard is unbalanced.

As shown in Fig. 2(a), the proposed sharding scheme keeps the number of cross-shard transactions around 10,000. Additionally, there is a transaction peak of around 14.05 million blocks. In the peak block, the random balanced sharding method generates 70,455 cross-shard transactions, while the unbalanced sharding method generates 54,629 cross-shard transactions. Community detection-based sharding generates only 14,972 cross-shard transactions, approximately one-fifth

---

[1] Due to the limited computational capacity, the local computer can only handle up to 90 addresses.

[2] 0x7be8076f4ea4a4ad08075c2508e481d6c946d12b, https://opensea.io/.

[3] 0x503828976d22510aad0201ac7ec88293211d23da, https://www.coinbase.com/.

[4] 0xd3d2e2692501a5c9ca623199d38826e513033a17, https://uniswap.org/.

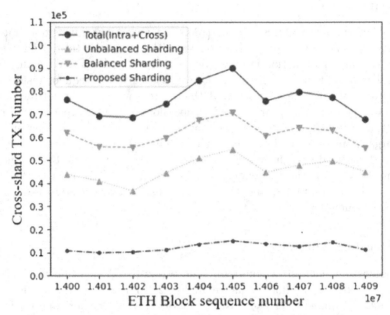

(a) Cross-shard TX Number, Community Detection VS Random Allocation

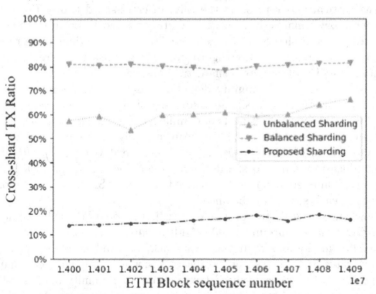

(b) Cross-shard TX Ratio, Community Detection VS Random Allocation

Fig. 2. Testing Ethereum address in sharding framework under unbalanced random allocation method, balanced random allocation method, and community detection-based allocation method while fixing tested addresses number $K = 90$ and shard number $s = 4$.

of the number generated by random sharding. With our proposed sharding technique, the peaks of shard lines appear relatively flat because it is based on a community detection algorithm. Figure 2(b) shows that random balanced and unbalanced sharding leads to a high ratio of cross-shard transactions, i.e., around 80% and 60% respectively. Compared with random sharding with balanced shards, the ratio of cross-shard transactions is reduced from 80% to 20% by implementing the community-detected sharding rather than random sharding.

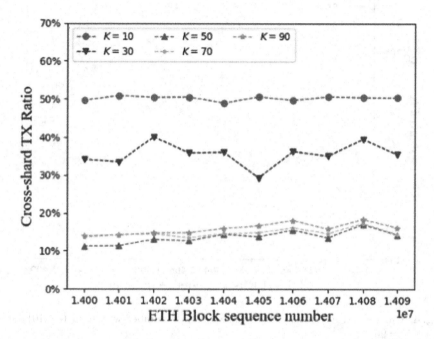

Fig. 3. Cross-shard TX ratio, the top 10 to 90 most traded addresses. Varying K within$\{10, 30, 50, 70, 90\}$, and fixing $s = 4$.

We explore our proposed scheme by changing the numbers of addresses or numbers of shards. According to Fig. 3, we demonstrate changes in the ratio of cross-shard transactions when the number of addresses varies. Table 2 presents the number of deleted addresses and the number of remaining addresses for each K value.

We evaluate our proposed community detection-based sharding approach by varying ETH most traded top K addresses from the range $\{10, 30, 50, 70, 90\}$ and fixing shard number $s = 4$. After traversing ten epochs, experiments on the ratio of ϕ_c in Fig. 3 reveal an interesting pattern of change. We see that a decrease in the ratio of ϕ_c occurs with an increase in K from 10 to 50, and an increase in the ratio of ϕ_c occurs with an increase in K from 50 to 90. The ratio of cross-shards is lowest when $K = 50$.

Table 2. Testes ETH top K addresses and remaining addresses

Tested ETH address number	$K=10$	$K=30$	$K=50$	$K=70$	$K=90$
Deleted address number	3	9	14	21	31
Remaining address number	7	21	36	49	59

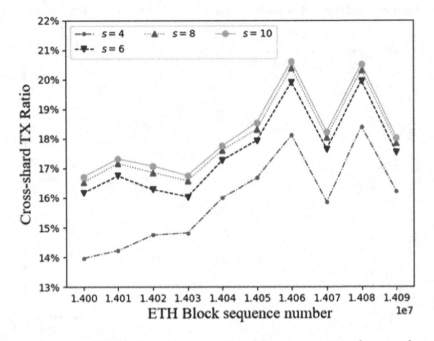

Fig. 4. Cross-shard TX ratio, while varying shards number within $\{4, 6, 8, 10\}$, and fixing $K = 90$.

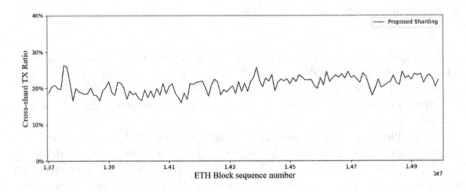

Fig. 5. Variation of cross-shard TX ratios in 1.3 million blocks.

In addition to varying the top K, we test sharding performance by changing the shard number s from the range $\{4, 6, 8, 10\}$ and fixed $K = 90$. The observation in Fig. 4 indicates that an increase in s leads to an increase in ϕ_c. Although the s increases with ϕ_c, the s and the ϕ_c do not follow a linear relationship. A significant change in the ratio of ϕ_c occurs when the s is increased from 4 to 6, followed by a continually smaller change as the s increases. Sharding results show that fewer shards result in a lower ratio of cross-shard transactions. Also, cross-shard transactions will reach upper bounds as more shards are added.

Figure 5 shows the test results of our proposed sharding method from the block range of 13.7 million to 15.04 million. We display the overall ratio of cross-shard transactions during the tested period. Community detection-based sharding reduces transactions between shards to 20% and stays stable.

5   Conclusion

We presented a community detection-based sharding scheme to reduce cross-shard transactions. We converted blockchain data into an undirected and weighted graph format and executed a community-detection algorithm to get communities. The assignment of nodes to communities represented the division of nodes into shards. The superiority of this sharding approach was demonstrated by evaluating it on a real-world Ethereum dataset. The community detection-based sharding scheme reduced the ratio of cross-shard transactions to 20% and maintained stability.

Acknowledgement. This work was supported by BT Group plc through the Project " *Blockchain based Workflow and Policy Management Platform*".

References

1. Nakamoto, S.: Bitcoin: a peer-to-peer electronic cash system. Decentralized Bus. Rev. 21260 (2008)
2. Wood, G., et al.: Ethereum: a secure decentralised generalised transaction ledger. Ethereum Proj. Yellow Pap. **151**(2014), 1–32 (2014)
3. Wang, X., et al.: Survey on blockchain for internet of things. Comput. Commun. **136**, 10–29 (2019)
4. Wang, X., Yu, G., Liu, R.P., et al.: Blockchain-enabled fish provenance and quality tracking system. IEEE Internet of Things J. **9**(11), 8130–8142 (2021)
5. Zhang, M., et al.: Go-sharing: a blockchain-based privacy-preserving framework for cross-social network photo sharing. IEEE Trans. Dependable Secure Comput. (2022)
6. Gerard, D.: Attack of the 50 Foot Blockchain: Bitcoin, Blockchain. Ethereum & smart contracts, David Gerard (2017)
7. Zhou, Q., Huang, H., Zheng, Z., Bian, J.: Solutions to scalability of blockchain: a survey. IEEE Access **8**, 16440–16455 (2020)

8. Wang, X., et al.: Capacity analysis of public blockchain. Comput. Commun. **177**, 112–124 (2021)
9. Luu, L., Narayanan, V., Zheng, C., Baweja, K., Gilbert, S., Saxena, P.: A secure sharding protocol for open blockchains. In: Proceedings of the 2016 ACM SIGSAC Conference on Computer and Communications Security, pp. 17–30 (2016)
10. Kokoris-Kogias, E., Jovanovic, P., Gasser, L., Gailly, N., Syta, E., Ford, B.: Omniledger: a secure, scale-out, decentralized ledger via sharding. In: 2018 IEEE Symposium on Security and Privacy (SP), pp. 583–598. IEEE (2018)
11. Zamani, M., Movahedi, M., Raykova, M.: Rapidchain: scaling blockchain via full sharding. In: Proceedings of the 2018 ACM SIGSAC Conference on Computer and Communications Security, pp. 931–948 (2018)
12. Wang, J., Wang, H.: Monoxide: scale out blockchains with asynchronous consensus zones. In: 16th USENIX Symposium on Networked Systems Design and Implementation (NSDI 19), pp. 95–112 (2019)
13. Al-Bassam, M., Sonnino, A., Bano, S., Hrycyszyn, D., Danezis, G.: Chainspace: a sharded smart contracts platform. arXiv preprint arXiv:1708.03778 (2017)
14. Yu, G., Wang, X., Yu, K., Ni, W., Zhang, J.A., Liu, R.P.: Survey: sharding in blockchains. IEEE Access **8**, 14155–14181 (2020)
15. Yu, G., Wang, X., Yu, K., Ni, W., Zhang, J.A., Liu, R.P.: Scaling-out blockchains with sharding: an extensive survey (2020)
16. Mearian, L.: Sharding: what it is and why many blockchain protocols rely on it (2019). https://www.computerworld.com/article/3336187/sharding-what-it-is-and-why-so-many-blockchain-protocols-rely-on-it.html. Accessed 2019
17. Zhang, M., Li, J., Chen, Z., Chen, H., Deng, X.: An efficient and robust committee structure for sharding blockchain. arXiv preprint arXiv:2112.15322 (2021)
18. Yu, G., Wang, X., Liu, R.P.: Cross-chain between a parent chain and multiple side chains. arXiv preprint arXiv:2208.05125, 2022
19. Liu, Y., Liu, J., Yin, J., Li, G., Yu, H., Wu, Q.: Cross-shard transaction processing in sharding blockchains. In: Qiu, M. (ed.) ICA3PP 2020. LNCS, vol. 12454, pp. 324–339. Springer, Cham (2020). https://doi.org/10.1007/978-3-030-60248-2_22
20. Awerbuch, B., Scheideler, C.: Robust random number generation for peer-to-peer systems. In: Shvartsman, M.M.A.A. (ed.) OPODIS 2006. LNCS, vol. 4305, pp. 275–289. Springer, Heidelberg (2006). https://doi.org/10.1007/11945529_20
21. Syta, E., et al.: Scalable bias-resistant distributed randomness. In: 2017 IEEE Symposium on Security and Privacy (SP), pp. 444–460. IEEE (2017)
22. Feldman, P.: A practical scheme for non-interactive verifiable secret sharing. In: 28th Annual Symposium on Foundations of Computer Science (sfcs 1987), pp. 427–438. IEEE (1987)
23. Sen, S., Freedman, M.J.: Commensal cuckoo: secure group partitioning for large-scale services. ACM SIGOPS Operating Syst. Rev. **46**(1), 33–39 (2012)
24. Androulaki, E., et al.: Hyperledger fabric: a distributed operating system for permissioned blockchains. In: Proceedings of the Thirteenth EuroSys Conference, pp. 1–15 (2018)
25. Androulaki, E., Cachin, C., De Caro, A., Kokoris-Kogias, E.: Channels: horizontal scaling and confidentiality on permissioned blockchains. In: Lopez, J., Zhou, J., Soriano, M. (eds.) ESORICS 2018. LNCS, vol. 11098, pp. 111–131. Springer, Cham (2018). https://doi.org/10.1007/978-3-319-99073-6_6

26. Kernighan, B.W., Lin, S.: An efficient heuristic procedure for partitioning graphs. Bell Syst. Tech. J. **49**(2), 291–307 (1970)
27. Blondel, V.D., Guillaume, J.L., Lambiotte, R., Lefebvre, E.: Fast unfolding of communities in large networks. J. Stat. Mech.: Theory Exp. **2008**(10), P10008 (2008)
28. Ankr.com. Build on Ethereum With Instant RPC Endpoint (2022). https://www.ankr.com/protocol/public/eth/. Accessed 2022

A Framework of Runtime Monitoring for Correct Execution of Smart Contracts

R. K. Shyamasundar[✉]

Department of Computer Science and Engineering, Indian Institute of Technology,
Bombay, Mumbai 400076, India
rkss@cse.iitb.ac.in

Abstract. Smart contracts have been subjected to several attacks that
have exploited various vulnerabilities of languages like Solidity, which
has resulted in huge financial losses. The functioning and deployment
of smart contracts are somewhat different from classical programming
environments. Once a smart contract is up and running, changing it,
is very complicated and nearly infeasible as the contract is expected to
be immutable when created. If we find a defect in a deployed smart
contract, a new version of the contract has to be created and deployed
with concurrence from the stakeholders. Further, when a new version
of an existing contract is deployed, data stored in the previous contract
does not get transferred automatically to the newly refined contract. We
have to manually initialize the new contract with the past data which
makes it very cumbersome and not very trustworthy. As neither updat-
ing a contract nor rolling back an update is possible, it greatly increases
the complexity of implementation and places a huge responsibility while
being deployed initially on the blockchain.

The main rationale for smart contracts has been to enforce contracts
safely among the stakeholders. In this paper, we shall discuss a framework
for runtime monitoring to prevent the exploitation of a major class of vulnerabilities using the programmers' annotations given in the smart contracts coded in Solidity. We have chosen several phrases for annotation
mimicking declarations of concurrent programming languages so that
the underlying run-time monitors can be automatically generated. The
annotations simply reflect the intended constraints on the execution of
programs relative to the object state relative to observables like method
calls, exceptions, etc. Such a framework further adds to the advantage of
debugging at the source level as the original structure is preserved and
also enhances the trust of the user as the run-time monitoring assertion
logs provide a rough *proof-outline* of the contract.

Keywords: Smart contract · Blockchain · EVM · Correctness ·
Debugging · Distributed programming languages · Object state

1 Introduction

The blockchain platform is a complex system consisting of nodes, network
devices, authentication services, dApps, wallets, web interfaces, key storage,

© The Author(s), under exclusive license to Springer Nature Switzerland AG 2022
S. Chen et al. (Eds.): ICBC 2022, LNCS 13733, pp. 92–116, 2022.
https://doi.org/10.1007/978-3-031-23495-8_7

miners, etc. It is a network of centralized and decentralized system components. Securing such a configuration is quite complex. The core technology of blockchain platforms is strongly secure as it satisfies properties like immutable, distributed, and public. However, in various use-case scenarios of the platforms, in particular dApps, the system is always a network of systems, and hence, it suffers from classic threats like data spoofing, data tampering, denial of service, privilege escalation, data-disclosure, neutralization of non-repudiation, etc. Security risks of such a system need to be treated in the traditional way. However, blockchain platforms evolving from Bitcoin have become highly flexible and expressively powerful due to the richness of underlying smart contracts. Smart contract languages today are derived from extensions of general-purpose languages like Javascript. While such a similarity makes smart contract languages look familiar to software developers, it is inadequate to accommodate domain-specific requirements of digital contracts. Smart contracts have not only shed light on the benefits of digital contracts but also on their potential risks. Smart contract languages like Solidity [30], GO [4], Clarity[1], Rust[2], DAML[3] etc., are widely used in practice. Like all software, smart contracts can contain bugs and their vulnerabilities can be exploited which can have direct financial consequences. Thus, it is very important to have a sound methodology, that is practical enough for use by a large community of smart contract programmers to check contracts for crucial properties. Quite a number of security vulnerabilities in smart contracts over Ethereum have been discovered [5] over the years and have been exploited extensively causing huge losses.

There has been a significant amount of work done in analyzing the correctness of smart contracts. A brief survey of the various approaches is given in Sect. 2.1. Broadly, the approaches use the following techniques to analyze the correctness of smart contracts: (1) symbolic execution-based static analysis/verification, (2) formal verification of smart contracts, (3) restricting the power of smart contract languages, (4) algorithmic analysis of the source- and the object-code (EVM), and (5) guidelines for the best practices. From a general programmer's perspective, it may be observed that (a) formal specification is hard; in particular, for dynamically-bound languages that require run-time checks on object's states, (b) the user prefers to debug at the source level rather than at the object level, (c) algorithmic analysis is limited, approximate, and has severe limitations due to over-/under-approximation, (d) several machine learning analyses have been post-detection and have a good amount of false positives, and (e) while the best practices serve the community extremely well, the lack of automatic tools to ascertain certain subtle advice comes in the way of gaining trust.

In this paper, we propose a framework for run-time monitoring through programmers' simple annotations that provide a trusted approach to prevent a major class of vulnerabilities from being exploited. Further, the approach has proposed a set of standard annotations that are similar to the declarative phrases

---

[1] https://book.clarity-lang.org.

[2] https://docs.casperlabs.io/dapp-dev-guide/writing-contracts/rust/.

[3] https://docs.daml.com/daml/reference/interfaces.html.

used in concurrent programming languages, which enables the prevention of a large number of vulnerabilities from being exploited. The main contributions of the paper are summarized below:

- Use of run-time monitoring to assure safe execution of smart contracts in Solidity, so that unintended executions with respect to the semantics of Solidity are prevented along with succinct error messages.
- Choice of annotation phrases parallels those that are used in the declarative part of a concurrent programming language and allows the prevention of a majority of vulnerabilities that are widely exploited. Such abstraction allows adapting source language compilations techniques to run-time monitoring.
- Use of run-time monitoring annotations to specify additional expressive constraints on complex/very expressive contracts.
- Automatic generation of run-time monitors from the given standard annotations and integrating the same with the smart contract source.
- Transforming the smart contract in Solidity with annotations to Solidity without annotations, preserving the semantics - leading to the capability of debugging the contract at the source level itself.

The rest of the paper is organized as follows: Sect. 2, provides an overview of smart contract vulnerabilities and a brief survey of the existing approaches to mitigate various vulnerabilities. Section 3 provides the salient aspects of the run-time monitoring framework. In Sects. 4 and 5, we discuss attack scenarios exploiting vulnerabilities followed by illustrations as to how such vulnerabilities are detected through run-time monitoring. In Sect. 6, we discuss how a majority of the vulnerabilities can be detected through standard annotations; in Sect. 6.3, it is shown how run-time monitors can be generated from the specified annotations for the given smart contract in Solidity. A comparative evaluation of the framework with those in the literature is carried out in Sect. 7. This is followed by conclusions in Sect. 8.

2   An Overview of Vulnerabilities in Smart Contracts

Serious fraud and the experience of smart contracts over the years have lead to the detection of several vulnerabilities. A spectrum of vulnerabilities that arise due to artifacts of Solidity, EVM, Blockchain structure, implicit distributed execution on a blockchain, etc., are discussed by several authors [5,32]. Vulnerabilities have been broadly classified into the following categories [5]:

1. Solidity Source Language Vulnerabilities: Some of the major vulnerabilities in this category are: re-entrancy, call to the unknown, gasless send, exception disorders, type casts, and transaction order dependence (partly due to the underlying blockchain), etc.,

2. Object Code (EVM) Vulnerabilities: Typical vulnerabilities[4] in this class are *ether* lost in the transfer, immutable bugs, etc., and

3. Blockchain-based Vulnerabilities: Major vulnerabilities in this class are generating randomness, unpredictable state, time constraints, etc.

2.1   Overcoming Smart Contract Exploits: A Brief Survey

There has been a significant amount of work in analyzing smart contracts for robustness. We can broadly classify the approaches into:

1. Static analysis based approaches [25,27,36]: Note that the characterization of vulnerabilities is quite often based on anecdotal incidents reported publicly. Luu et al. [25] present a symbolic execution tool for analyzing smart contracts at the bytecode level. The system requires an analysis of best-effort manual analysis of the EVM bytecode to characterize the security bugs in the program as a trace using constraint solver $Z3$ to eliminate infeasible traces. The tool leads to various false positives and a recent analysis [16] has shown that the verification conditions generated by it are neither sound nor complete. MPro [36] is another efficient and scalable tool that combines symbolic execution and data dependency analysis thus reducing false positives.

2. Transformation of Smart contracts: One of the early works [6], uses a two-way language-based approach for verifying smart contracts. They translate the contracts written in a subset of EVM to F*-a functional programming language with the aim of program verification. The subset is quite limited and there is no evidence that it can capture a large fraction of real-life smart contracts. Securify [35] is a lightweight security verifier for Ethereum smart contracts. It uses a new domain-specific language, Securify, that enables users to express new vulnerability patterns as they emerge. To check these patterns, Securify symbolically encodes the dependence graph of the contract in stratified Datalog and leverages off-the-shelf Datalog solvers for efficient analysis of the code. Securify derives semantic facts inferred by analyzing the contracts dependency graph and uses these facts to check a set of compliance and violation patterns. Based on the outcome of these checks, Securify classifies all contract behaviors into violations, warnings, and compliant ones. Again, there is a lot of expertise required in formulating patterns and as such arriving at patterns of complex interaction is not quite simple for a naive programmer.

3. Formal correctness, formal semantic frameworks for Solidity cum EVM: Approaches on these lines are explored in [2,10,13,16,20,21,29]. In [10] an approach for proof-carrying smart contracts is explored through an example of ERC20 treating a smart contract as a distributed program. In a theorem-proving-based approach, one is concerned with the verification of the semantic specification of EVM bytecode of the contract using several standard frameworks like *Coq, Isabelle, Why3* etc. In [15], the authors propose techniques

---

[4] Compiler limits like *Stack size limit* can also be exploited by adversaries but the current compilers have overcome such exploits.

and tools for a formal characterization of smart contracts and static analysis of EVM bytecode. Another interesting tool is the automated static analyzer called eThor [31] for EVM bytecode that is shown to be sound. VERX [29] is another automated verifier of functional requirements for Ethereum smart contracts.

4. New sound programming languages: [8] introduces Featherweight Solidity, a calculus formalizing the core features of the Solidity language, thus providing a fundamental step to reason about the safety properties of smart contracts' source code. Such an approach prevents some errors whereas many others, such as accesses to a nonexisting function or state variable, are only detected at the run-time and cause interruption and roll-back of transactions. A linear logic-based approach has been envisaged in [9] for abstracting resource-aware session types in the specification of smart contracts.

5. Platforms for good (defensive!) practices: Manticore[5] is an open-source tool that can explore the reachability of states having its own method of specification. Further, there has been a spectrum of guidelines/practices from industries in building smart contracts. One such approach is DappGuard [24] which provides an initial design for live monitoring based on the authors' findings on various smart contracts. MYTHRIL [26] is a service platform for Ethereum to assist programmers to avoid costly errors.

A qualitative comparative evaluation is carried out in Sect. 7.

3   Runtime Monitoring Framework: A Rationale

In formal verification of imperative programs, one establishes correctness statically by showing that the program execution satisfies the specification in all the plausible execution paths relative to the specification that include pre-/post-conditions, and invariants/assertions at various control points of the program. In the context of declarative languages, while partial correctness is implicit in the program itself, it often requires proof of termination [23]. Solidity is a rich expressive imperative language used for writing smart contracts that naturally depends on dynamic binding due to the underlying blockchain structure. While formal specification/verification of distributed programs is itself quite complex, the dynamic binding of variables and the functions/methods that get executed on the blockchain makes it much more complex. Our run-time framework is structured to monitor smart contracts using the following rationale:

1. Quite a number of vulnerabilities arise due to the dynamic nature of method binding including fallback functions. Our approach is to use run-time monitors to eliminate incorrect execution paths in line with the semantics of Solidity.

2. Run-time monitoring to control the execution traces in alignment with the sequential requirement of execution of the underlying distributed program.

---

[5] GitHub - trailofbits/manticore: Symbolic execution tool.

3. Run-time monitor for exceptions by appropriately composing SafeMath for general expressions.
4. Run-time monitor for user-defined assertions to satisfy the requirements of smart contracts.

In the next section, we shall illustrate the above rationale through an illustration of the detection of a few major vulnerabilities and their mitigation through run-time monitoring.

4 Run-Time Monitors to Prevent Unintended Execution Traces

In this section, we shall look at two major vulnerabilities (a) Re-entrancy and (b) Transaction order indeterminacy that has been responsible for siphoning a sizable amount of crypto-currency.

4.1 Attacks Due to Re-entrancy Vulnerability

The property of non-re-entrancy can be interpreted as follows: *When a non-recursive function is invoked, it cannot re-enter before its termination. This is a requirement, a programmer takes it for granted due to the sequentiality and atomicity requirements of transactions. But this is not always true due to the fallback mechanism.* The well-known DAO attack which happened to steal a large amount of money was due to the re-entrancy vulnerability. The attack comes in two variants that are illustrated below.

SimpleDAO: Attack1. Consider the simple DAO shown in Fig. 1 and the attacker code shown in Fig. 2. Steps are given below that capture the scenario of the attack:

1. Publish contract Mallory2 with address "xyz".
2. Assume Mallory2 donates 100 ethers to SimpleDAO i.e., credit["xyz"] = 100.
3. Let the adversary account be at address "123".
4. "123" transfers 100 ethers to "xyz". This invokes the fallback function of Mallory, which internally invokes withdraw function of DAO with amount = 100.
5. msg.sender.call.value(amount)() invokes the fallback function of Mallory2.
6. The credit of Mallory2 will never be changed and thus, all the money from DAO will be transferred to Mallory2 (even if Mallory2 invested only 100 Ethers in DAO).
7. This recursive execution will continue till: a) the gas is exhausted, or b) the balance of DAO becomes 0.

```
 3 ▾ contract SimpleDAO {
 4       mapping (address => uint256) public credit;
 5
 6 ▾     constructor() payable public {
 7           donate();
 8       }
 9
10 ▾     function donate() payable public{
11           credit[msg.sender] += msg.value;
12       }
13
14 ▾     function withdraw(uint256 amount) public{
15 ▾         if (credit[msg.sender]>= amount) {
16               msg.sender.call.value(amount)("");
17               credit[msg.sender]-=amount;
18           }
19       }
20
21 ▾     function queryCredit(address to) public view returns (uint256) {
22           return credit[to];
23       }
24   }
```

Fig. 1. Original SimpleDAO

```
26 ▾ contract Mallory2 {
27       SimpleDAO public dao;
28       address payable owner;
29
30 ▾     constructor(SimpleDAO addr) public payable{
31         owner = msg.sender;
32         dao = addr;
33       }
34
35 ▾     function attack() public payable{
36         dao.donate.value(1)();
37         dao.withdraw(1);
38       }
39
40 ▾     function getJackpot() public{
41         dao.withdraw(address(dao).balance);
42         owner.transfer(address(this).balance);
43       }
44
45 ▾     function() external payable{
46         dao.withdraw(1);
47       }
48   }
```

Fig. 2. Attacker contract Mallory2

The attack was possible due to the fact that `withdraw()` - a non-recursive function that was expected to be non-re-entrant, re-entered itself before termination due to the fallback call[6]. The execution violated the underlying semantics and succeeded in getting into the attacker's fallback function. In fact, Solidity document [12] gives the following warning: "Any interaction with another contract imposes a potential danger, especially if the source code of the contract is not known in advance. The current contract hands over control to the called contract and that may potentially do just about anything. Even if the called contract inherits from a known parent contract, the inheriting contract is only required to have a correct interface. The implementation of the contract, however, can be completely arbitrary and thus, poses a danger. In addition, be prepared in case it calls into other contracts of your system or even back into the calling contract before the first call returns. This means that the called contract can change the state variables of the calling contract via its functions. Write your functions in a way that, for example, calls to external functions happen after many changes to state variables in your contract so that your contract is not vulnerable to an exploit". It must be noted that simpleDAO is already on the blockchain, and hence, it is not feasible to predict future user contracts like Mallory2.

```
1 contract Mallory3 {
2 SimpleDAO public dao = SimpleDAO(0x818EA...);
3 address owner; bool performAttack = true;
4
5 function Mallory3(){ owner = msg.sender; }
6
7 function attack() {
8 dao.donate.value(1)(this);
9 dao.withdraw(1);
10 }
```

```
1 function() {
2 if (performAttack) {
3 performAttack = false;
4 dao.withdraw(1);
5 }}
6
7 function getJackpot(){
8 dao.withdraw(dao.balance);
9 owner.send(this.balance);
10 }}
```

Fig. 3. Mallory3 contract for Attack2

SimpleDAO: Attack2. Now consider the SimpleDAO shown in Fig. 1 and the attacker *Mallory3* shown in Fig. 3. The second attack described in [5] is more subtle and allows an adversary to steal all the *ether* from SimpleDAO, with only two calls to the fallback function. Such an attack is realized through a new contract: Mallory3 contract shown in Fig. 3 where one donates just 1 *wie* to the SimpleDAO contract. After donating 1 *wie*, the attacker can then `withdraw` 1 *wie* using `withdraw` function. The `withdraw` function sends 1 *wie* back and calls *fallback* function of Mallory3 contract, which calls *withdraw* function again. After the second call, the stack begins to unwind. While unwinding first the balance

---

[6] The requirement for run-time checks for overcoming the re-entrancy vulnerability follows from the decidability issues of the problem of effective call-back free contracts discussed in [17] where the general problem is shown to be undecidable in Turing-complete languages.

is updated by 0 (zero) and the second time by $2^{256} - 1$ *wei* due to underflow. This allows attackers to steal everything from SimpleDAO. Finally, Mallory3 invokes getJackpot, which steals all the ether from SimpleDAO, and transfers it to Mallory3.

4.2   Mitigation for Attack1 on SimpleDAO

```
string[] callStack; //Injected code

function withdraw(uint256 amount) public{
    checkReentrancy("withdraw"); //Injected code
    callStack.push("withdraw"); //Injected code

    if (credit[msg.sender]>= amount) {
        msg.sender.call.value(amount)("");
        credit[msg.sender]-=amount;
    }

    delete callStack[callStack.length-1]; //Injected code
    callStack.length--; //Injected code
}

//Injected function
function checkReentrancy(string memory functionName) public {
    uint flag;
    if(callStack.length > 0){
        for(uint i=callStack.length; i>0; i--) {
            if(keccak256(abi.encodePacked(callStack[i-1]))==
            keccak256(abi.encodePacked(functionName))) {
                flag = 0;
                break;
            }
        }
    } else {
        flag = 1;
    }

    require(flag==1, "Reentrant!!");
}
```

Fig. 4. Modified SimpleDAO to overcome re-entrancy (Attack1)

In the simpleDAO problem, the function "withdraw" is expected to be non-re-entrant. One simple approach is to instrument the program with run-time checks so that the re-entrancy of "withdraw" is detected and prevented from executing further. The transformed program with only the relevant code snippet is shown

in Fig. 4 which introduces run-time checks in the original DAO program shown
in Fig. 1. The modified instrumentation is given below:

1. The new injected function **checkReentrancy** checks for re-entrancy of a call
   by book-keeping the call-stack for re-entrant calls; the re-entrancy is detected
   by flag through the **require** statement in **checkReentrancy**.
2. In functions **withdraw**, the **callstack.push** is introduced to keep track of
   the new call and the call stack is popped out on exiting the procedure, and a
   flag is set on re-entrancy.
3. It is to be noted the monitors are checking the conditions on the object state
   at run-time.

4.3   Mitigation for Attack2 on SimpleDAO

From the description given in Sect. 4.3, and Fig. 3, we need to overcome the
following two issues:

1. Re-entrancy of **withdraw**: The remedial measure for the re-entrancy can be
   taken on the lines of the mitigation shown in Fig. 4.
2. Exception Handling for overflow/underflow while reducing the amount after
   getting the funds back can be done using the technique of SafeMath [28] for
   recent versions of Solidity[7]. For instance, in the context of unsigned integer
   arithmetic, the code snippet for subtraction is given below:

```
function sub(uint256 a, uint256 b) internal pure returns (unint256) {
  require(b<= a, "safemath:Subtraction Overflow");
  uint256 c = a -b;
  return c;
  }
```

3. In context of context of **withdraw**, its last line gets replaced by

$$\text{credit[msg.sender]= SafeMath.sub(credit[msg.sender], amount)}$$

5   Run-Time Monitoring to Control Execution Traces

Even though EVM execution is single-threaded, transactions are submitted in
parallel, and miners may reorder and interleave those transactions arbitrarily [10,
32]. For this reason, it is possible to have data races as well as nondeterministic
transaction orders. These are illustrated through two examples in the following.

---

[7] SafeMath transforms expressions in a binary manner. That is, for exception handling
in compound expressions, say, for instance, a + b + c, SafeMath needs to be invoked
compositionally.

5.1   Transaction Order Nondeterminism Issue

Figure 5, shows a simple Solidity contract GetterSetter containing two functions. get function allows a user to query the contract for the balance and the set function allows a user to update the balance with the value passed as an argument and return the old value of the balance. If this contract is concurrently executed by two customers, the answer would be non-deterministic. For instance, consider the following two scenarios:

Scenario 1:
  1. C1 calls set(100); C1 calls get(); - returns 100
  2. C2 calls set(50); C2 calls get(); - returns 50
Scenario 2:
  1. C1 calls set(100); C2 calls set(50);
  2. C1 calls get(); - returns 50
  3. C2 calls get(); - returns 50 Nondeterminism depicted in (Scenario 2) is
     essentially due to interleaving of operations of transactions.

```
3 ▾ contract GetterSetter {
4        uint private balance;
5
6 ▾      function get() public returns(uint) {
7            return balance;
8        }
9
10 ▾     function set(uint x) public returns(uint) {
11           uint t = balance;
12           balance = x;
13           return t;
14       }
15  }
```

Fig. 5. Original getter setter contract

5.2   Overcoming Transaction Order Dependency

Here, the pattern for vulnerability is due to data races that could be avoided by taking into account the accessibility of the procedures of the contracts and also understanding the concurrent procedures that can co-exist without interfering with each other. The transformed body-part of Solidity is shown in Fig. 6 considering the access pattern: (GET SET); that is, set can be accessed by a process only after[8] a get. Let us assume several processes can call get in a concurrent

---

[8] This is a constraint we have enforced for simplicity; we could enforce controls like only one writer is permitted on a shared resource whereas multiple readers are allowed on that shared resource. This will become clear when we discuss nondeterminism in ERC20.

```
3 ▾  contract GetterSetter {
4         uint private balance;
5         mapping (address => string) public lastCall;
6
7 ▾      function get() public returns(uint) {
8             lastCall[msg.sender] = "get";
9             return balance;
10        }
11
12 ▾     function set(uint x) public returns(uint) {
13            require(keccak256(abi.encodePacked(lastCall[msg.sender]))
14            ==keccak256(abi.encodePacked("get")),
15            "set() should be called after get()");
16            lastCall[msg.sender] = "set";
17            uint t = balance;
18            balance = x;
19            return t;
20        }
21   }
```

Fig. 6. Getter setter with access control

```
3 ▾  contract GetterSetter {
4         uint private balance;
5         address lastGetCalled;
6         mapping (address => string) public lastCall;
7
8 ▾      function get() public returns(uint) {
9             require((lastGetCalled==address(0x0) || lastGetCalled==msg.sender),
10            "concurrent execution by another contract!");
11            lastGetCalled = msg.sender;
12            lastCall[msg.sender] = "get";
13            return balance;
14        }
15
16 ▾     function set(uint x) public returns(uint) {
17            require(lastGetCalled==msg.sender,
18            "concurrent execution by another contract!");
19            require(keccak256(abi.encodePacked(lastCall[msg.sender]))
20            ==keccak256(abi.encodePacked("get")),
21            "set() should be called after get()");
22            lastCall[msg.sender] = "set";
23            uint t = balance;
24            balance = x;
25            lastGetCalled = address(0x0);
26            return t;
27        }
28   }
```

Fig. 7. Getter setter with concurrency & access control

fashion (note that multiple reading does not interfere with each other). Figure 6 and Fig. 7 show runtime checks (on the object-state) introduced in the body of Solidity shown in Fig. 5 so that access of actions is as per requirement.

5.3   ERC20 Token Standard and Issues of Nondeterminism

A large number of Ethereum development standards focus on token interfaces that help in ensuring the composable nature of smart contracts. ERC20 is the earliest token standard by Ethereum. Its brief interface[9] specification[10] is given below:

1. functions totalSupply(), balanceOf(address account), allowance () as well as emit events do not change the state.
2. `function transfer(address recipient, uint256 amount) external returns (bool)`: transfers a specified number of tokens from the caller to a different address (and reduces the balance of tokens by that quantity) if available. The `transfer` function is called to transfer tokens from the sender's account to a different one and it returns a boolean value, that is always true.
3. `function approve(address spender, uint256 amount) external returns (bool)`: It grants an allowance for another user. Note that there is no requirement that the sender should have at least the number of tokens granted at that time (or even later).
4. `function transferFrom(address sender, address recipient, uint256 amount) external returns (bool)`; i.e., `transferFrom` is used by the grantee to spend the allowance that has been approved earlier by some other user or owner for it.
   - Functionally, the operation (i) transfers an amount less than or equal to the allowance that has been approved by some other owner/user, (ii) and reduces the allowance by that amount, and (iii) the operation fails if the amount to be transferred is greater than the approved allowance (if that happens, it reverts).
   - It is this function along with `approve` that leads to possible misuse.

Remarks: The main differences between `transfer` and `transferFrom` are:

- In the case of `transfer`, the owner of the account grants certain number tokens to others. Thus, book keeping of the tokens can be done exclusively by the owner and there is no need of others to interfere. *Note that in an asynchronous system, the owner of a resource can control the order of his own transactions but not control the order of transaction of other users.*
- While in the case of `transferFrom`, the book keeping of the tokens cannot be done exclusively by the owner; the others (grantees by the owner) have to assist in book keeping as and when they use the partial or the full grant. Semantically, it can be interpreted as an account (or variable) that can be modified by multiple accounts/users; for a more detailed discussion the reader is referred to [33]. The issue with multiple users writing onto one account becomes clear in the sequel.

---

[9] https://ethereum.org/en/developers/docs/standards/tokens/erc-20/.
[10] https://ethereum.org/en/developers/tutorials/erc20-annotated-code/.

Attacks Scenario in ERC20. Consider a scenario of users (say owners of accounts) $\{U_1, U_2, \cdots, U_n\}$. Let $A_{ij} \; \forall i \neq j$ be the `Allowance` approved by U_i to users $U_j, \forall i \neq j$. It is to be noted users $\{U_1, U_2, \cdots, U_n\}$ are to be treated as asynchronous or loosely coupled processes. Possible attack scenario on ERC20 are well-documented[11]. A basic attack scenario is described below:

1. U_1 approves 80 tokens to U_2 (i.e., U_{12} is 80)
2. U_1 realises that he made mistake and he should have approved only 50 tokens.
3. To correct the mistake, U_1 sends out an approval using `Approve` for 50 tokens to U_2.
4. Now there are following two possibilities:
   (a) It is possible that U_2 has already withdrawn x tokens, $0 \leq x \leq 80$, using `transferFrom`. Thus U_2 will get additional 50 tokens, over and above x.
   (b) If U_2 is still to transfer, then the allowance U_{12} will get set to 50 tokens as wanted by U_1 perhaps (assuming he had done a mistake).

The basic reason for such an anomalous behaviour is that users $\{U_1, U_2, \cdots, U_n\}$ are asynchronous and hence lead to nondeterminism as the program does not use either a locks or a synchronization construct. A general programmer understands that the execution on blockchains like Ethereum using smart contracts is sequential and thus, does not realize the underlying nondeterminism that could arise due to interleaving of method calls. This is nicely illustrated in [22], where a following parallel is drawn:

> Accounts using smart contracts in a blockchain are like threads using concurrent objects in shared memory with correspondences of artifacts as below: *contract state to object state, call/send to context switching, Reentrancy to (Un)cooperative multitasking, Invariants to Atomicity and Nondeterminism to Data races.*

While one could have illustrated the attack scenario using only two users, we introduced n users to understand the general complexity. We can observe from the interface:

1. `transfer` can be interpreted as follows: The user say U_i transfers to some other account $U_j, j \neq i$. This corresponds to the owner sending his tokens to other accounts. Looking at the function in an isolated manner, it is like its storage is written only by himself (owner) and nobody else.
2. `transferFrom` can be interpreted as follows: Here, user U_i, takes $x \leq U_{ji}$ tokens (allowed by Owner U_j to U_i), and transfers to some other user U_k, $i, k \neq j$. Thus, U_i writes into the storage owned by U_j.
3. Looking at (1)–(2) above, we can see the storage of U_i is being written by the other processes (grantees of U_j) as well. If we treat each of the account of U_i as an asset, one can see that each account in principle can be written by other accounts/users who are not its owners. In other words, the abstraction of the

---

[11] https://docs.google.com/document/d/1YLPtQxZu1UAvO9cZ1O2RPXBbT0mooh 4DYKjA_jp-RLM/edit\#.

stakeholders can be seen as an n-shared asset problem discussed in [4,18] using a slight variation of ERC20 standard. In fact, the authors of [4] show that n-shared asset problem (hence ERC20) requires strong synchronization requiring consensus rather than just atomic registers and show that the bound on consensus number is dependant on the *object state* at that instant.

4. Overlaying the use of `approve` together with (1)–(3) provides a complete picture of execution of ERC20 usage in a given deployed context.

Thus, to establish the correctness of ERC20 deployment, we not only have to show that the attack scenario relative to `approve` is not possible but also show that the execution traces arising from (1)–(2) above also do not introduce any new attack scenarios.

To prevent such interleaving executions, the run-time monitor approach discussed in Sect. 5.2 can be adapted. Informally speaking, we need to assure, non-interfering execution of the various methods `approve()`, `transfer()` and `transferFrom()` instantiated from the users. This could be done through clauses ACCESS and PARALLEL discussed above or INVAR discussed in Sect. 6.3. It may be noted that realizing the clauses need to track the object state at that instant. For lack of space, we shall not go into details here; for further discussions, the reader is referred to [33].

6   Realizing Run-Time Monitors Through Annotations

In this section, we shall first discuss how the user specifies the annotations and indicate those that could be treated as standard, the basis of generating run-time monitors automatically from annotations and the scope of annotations in the context of smart contracts.

6.1   Annotations for Solidity Contracts and Standard Annotations

In the previous sections, we have illustrated various scenarios showing the exploitation of vulnerabilities like re-entrancy through the DAO, transaction order indeterminacy, nondeterminism in ERC20 tokens, and shown how run-time monitoring can be used to prevent exploitation of the underlying vulnerabilities. Now, a question arises:

> Is it the case that every time the programmer has to arrive at the run-time monitoring code? or Is there a general methodology to generate the run-time monitors automatically?

In the following we illustrate, as to how the programmer can specify the annotations.

6.2   Specification of Annotations

The programmer need not have to write the run-time monitoring code but just annotate the methods or expressions. With such annotations, the run-time monitors can be automatically generated and integrated with the smart contracts. We shall illustrate typical annotations for the vulnerabilities discussed above and these will be treated as **standard annotations**.

A. *Annotation for Simple DAO - Attack1*: The main problem has been the re-entrancy in `withdraw`. The suggested annotation is:

NON-REENTRANT withdraw()

 – Interpretation: Prevent `withdraw` from re-entrancy at run-time.

B. *Annotation for Simple DAO - Attack2*: The main problem has been the re-entrancy of `withdraw` method as well as the overflow of the decrement expression. The annotation to be provided is:

NON-REENTRANT withdraw()

SafeMath (credit[msg.sender]-=amount)

 – while the first one is the same as above, the second one says the expression `credit[msg.sender]-=amount` should be run-time checked for arithmetic overflow and underflow.

C. *Annotation for Getter Setter Contract*: It has two annotations:
  1. `ACCESS (get), (get set)`
     – ACCESS annotation describes the execution order of calls of methods for each process (user). It essentially describes the trace of the possible method calls in the execution traces. In the annotation above, it is interpreted as a call to `get` or if `set` is called it has to be preceded by a `get`; in fact one could use regular expressions for specifying the access patterns [7] over method signatures. In a sense, the regular expression form could be: get* ∪ (get set)*. The interpretation is an user can call repeatedly `get` or follow the pattern of, first `get` and then `set` repeatedly.
  2. `PARALLEL (get get), (get set)`
     – The interpretation is: `get` can be called by several users possibly concurrently but at most one user can schedule `set` at any time subjected to the constraints specified in the ACCESS annotation.

Remarks: *A general question is: Why not realize "re-entrancy" or arithmetic exceptions for all the methods or expressions?* As Solidity execution requires gas, one need to monitor only where needed; one approach could be to first use it in general and debug the program through assertions to eliminate those that do not require run-time checks.

6.3 Generating Run-Time Monitors from Standard Annotations

From Sects. 4.2, 4.3, and 5.2, it is easy to see that the annotations as specified above can indeed generate the guards and the respective code-snippets for the checking. However, we shall illustrate below that the annotations can be treated as declarations and then the run-time monitors are generated similar to the run-time checks introduced by the compilers in classical concurrent programming languages.

6.4   Declarations in a Shared Variable Programming Language

Our method of generating run-time monitors from standard annotations is based on the technique of *DECLARATIONS* used in concurrent programming languages to specify constraints on the execution of the program (used by the compiler to appropriately generate static/run-time checks as the case may be).

Programming languages for concurrent and distributed computing was one of key areas of research in 1980's [19]. The main rationale of specification (declaration) section of a concurrent program was meant to capture the interaction of processes [3,34] and the interaction of shared resources with processes. According to [3] concurrent programming languages have the following four important goals: expressiveness, data integrity, security and verifiability [3]. There have been a variety of concurrent programming languages keeping the discussed rationale. In early stages, languages were designed keeping in view the correctness -usually realized through discipline in usage either through formal specification or through formal declarations clauses. For instance, one of the early well designed languages, Ada, was quite disciplined from a concurrent perspective; here integrity was realized through mutual exclusive access of shared resources. For this reason, Ada rendezvous was considered inefficient as it did not permit concurrency even when the operations were non-interfering. There have been lot of research to realize efficiency/performance without foregoing correctness. For instance [34] explored a language structure to realize data integrity without unnecessary mutual exclusion. A typical shared variable program is a set of processes and shared resources and its structure is depicted in Fig. 8.

Clauses Import/Export highlight resources/services that can be imported or exported. The clause INVAR highlights the invariant property of the underlying resources. Clauses in the section CONSTRAINTS, vary based on the permitted interaction of processes and access of shared resources. For instance [34] requisite declarative clauses have been introduced so that data integrity can be realized without enforcing mutual exclusion unnecessarily and a methodology of establishing formal correctness through interference freedom proofs among processes and resources under the given constraints is described. The section 'Trans' highlights the operations that are possible on the resource. The MOD-BODY describes implementation of the operations. Further, the correctness of the program with classes ACCESS, or PARALLEL is established in [34].

Generating Run-Time Monitors

It is easy to see that the approach of DECLARATIONS highlighted above can be adapted for smart contracts by observing the similarity between the smart contract and the shared variable program. The authors of [22,32] have nicely demonstrated the similarity of smart contracts with that of a distributed programming structure through the following parallels: accounts using smart contracts in a

```
Process <process name ... >
Import ....          (* Classical syntax *)
Body
end Process


MODSPEC Shared < Resource name>
IMPORT < components being imported into the Module>
Export < components being expored outside the Module>
INVAR  < invariance on resource>
NONRENTRANT (...)  (* This is the additional clause for smart contracts *)
PARALLEL (...) (* Lists methods that could be instantiated concurrently *)
ACCESS (...)   (* Regular expressions on operations that provide the
                                          trace structure *)
CONSTRAINTS  (*for interaction among processes and    resources
                            Is specified in varied forms  *)
Trans    (* various operations/functions/procedures that operate
                  On the resource *)
Entry procedure p1 (...)
Entry procedure p2 (...)
...
Entry procedure p2 (...)
end ModSPEC
```

Fig. 8. General structure of a distributed program

blockchain are like threads using concurrent objects in shared memory, contract state with object state, call/send with context switching, re-entrancy with (un)-cooperative multi-tasking. Thus, now we can use the same technique with additional clause like REENTRANT for smart contracts; note that re-entrancy does not happen in classical languages as there is no fallback function.

For standard annotations discussed above, NON- REENTRANT, ACCESS, PARALLEL, by looking at the original Solidity contract and the Modified Solidity contract, it should become clear that based on the declarations and the information in the contract, the run-time monitors can be generated. We shall not discuss the algorithms here due to lack of space. We have built a pre-processor[12] for Solidity with *Annotations*, using the comment structure, that transforms it into a semantic preserving Solidity program satisfying by the declarations both statically and at run-time. The structure of the system is depicted in Fig. 9. The translation essentially uses the semantics of the respective annotation as an additional method of the contract and transforms the original program by guarded execution of the methods using the constructs like require, revert of Solidity as needed (we have also used assert statement as well for purpose of debugging). The method corresponding to the semantics of the annotation clause shall have the abstraction of events that are needed for guard expres-

---

[12] Snehal Borse, Prateek Patidar Solidity+: Specification Enhanced Solidity to Overcome Vulnerabilities, M.Tech. Dissertation, Department of Computer Science and Engineering, IIT Bombay 2019.

sions. Note that the structure of the transformed program remains unchanged, and hence, debugging the original program and the transformed program can be done with the same ease by the programmer; this is quite apparent from our earlier illustrations.

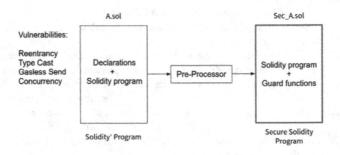

Fig. 9. Transformer for solidity program with declarations

Scope of the Approach

We have applied the approach to a large number of contracts that have vulnerabilities like re-entrancy, exceptions, type cast, gasless send, block.timestamp, Tx.origin, transaction order dependency etc., and successfully executed the contracts preventing the vulnerabilities being exploited.

Even though our approach is run-time oriented, we wanted to compare with various tools, even if they are static analysis based, to get a view of the utility and also the claim on the naturalness of debugging at the source level. For this purpose, we evaluated our system with Mythril[13] – a tool targeted to detect common vulnerabilities including integer underflow, owner-overwrite-to-Ether-withdrawal, etc., using symbolic executors (that may even be unsound often as the exploration space is limited) through bug injection in programs. We took a sample of 50 benchmark smart contracts [14] and found that our approach detects all those errors with succinct error messages apart from handling run-time errors as illustrated.

There are several programming tricks used by programmers to realize randomness or enforce time constraints, mismatch of interpretation of private/public for realizing secrecy. These errors have also been able to handle through guarded execution through the user annotations.

Another major vulnerability is that of *ether lost in transfer* - loss of *ether* happens when *ether* is sent to killed contracts or unknown addresses. This happens due to the underlying semantics of Solidity. One of the well known attacks exploiting such a vulnerability is the Parity fiasco (1-Parity and 2-Parity errors) [1]. As the general problem of detecting such losses is generally undecidable, the authors [27] have built a static analysis tool called, MAIAN, that

---

[13] https://mythril-classic.readthedocs.io/en/master/about.html.

classifies vulnerabilities into greedy, prodigal, suicidal, and posthumous statically. Our run-time framework could be used by annotating the *owners* in the contract and prevent a majority of such losses.

More Expressive Contracts. *Conditional Requirements*: Let us consider a conditional requirements like: *B can send Y to C only if it has received X from A.* It should be easy to see that the ACCESS class can be used to specify the appropriate annotation. This class of contracts are in general difficult to handle and often seen as anomalous behaviour of the blockchain execution.

General Enforcement of Constraints: Runtime verification approaches like specifying constraints using automata and timers have been explored in [11]. For instance, consider the first three clauses of the general English language contract taken from an interface description in [11].

1. The casino owner may deposit or withdraw money from the casino's bank, with the bank's balance never falling below zero.
2. As long as no game is in progress, the owner of the casino may make available a new game by tossing a coin and hiding its outcome. The owner must also set a participation cost of their choice for the game.
3. Clauses 1 and 2 are constrained in that as long as a game is in progress, the bank balance may never be less than the sum of the participation cost of the game and its win-out.

In [11], the programmer need to specify the requirements in a specification language LARVA that generates the needed run-time monitor. In our approach, noting that the constraint specified in (3), i.e., *as long as a game is in progress, bank balance may never be less than the sum of the participation cost of the game and its win-out* becomes the INVAR described in Fig. 8. Note that INVAR is an invariance of the contract and guarded execution of methods can be written using annotations like $at(method1)->Cond1$, where $at(methdod1)$ denotes that the control point of the program at the beginning of *method1*; similarly $after(method1)$ denoted the control point after the completion of the body of method1. It can be easily seen, that programmer will find it easy to specify such annotations using INVAR that will be distributed over the methods by our preprocessor to make sure that the condition holds true always. For lack of space, we shall not go into further details.

Clause 3 of the legal contract says: "as long as a game is in progress, the bank balance may never be less than the sum of the participation cost of the game and its win-out." To ensure that Clause 3 holds we need to guard the function withdraw to maintain condition as an invariance (can be captured through the INVAR clause) as also other accessed functions.

7   A Comparative Discussion

We have explored a large number of smart contracts and instrumented them to check/validate their behaviour during execution. In particular, typical contracts with vulnerabilities underlying standard annotations explored earlier like re-entrancy (DAO Attack 1 or Attack2, unknown caller), type cast, transaction order nondeterminism (ERC20, getter-setter), exceptions, etc., when executed are prevented from executing the contract further with appropriate exceptions and error messages to the user. Vulnerabilities such as unchecked send, gasless send are also being handled through annotations at the respective points. We have integrated our runtime monitor with a symbolic executor that provides a trace that would contain these assertions while passing through the remix debugger.

There is yet another set of vulnerabilities that has caught attention through the Parity Multisig attacks (Parity-1 and Parity-2) like characterizing prodigal, suicidal, greedy, posthumous contracts [27]. As already mentioned, a majority of the losses due to such vulnerabilities can be captured in our run-time framework using annotations about the owner, users who can change the ownerships etc. Such an enrichment is being experimented in our new prototype being engineered in Python by Hrishikesh Saloi, and Mohammad Ummair, at IIT Bombay.

Compared to transformational approaches [6,35], our approach works on full language without resorting to EVM level. Proof-theoretic approaches [2,10,13, 16,20,21,29] that work on Solidity cum EVM have their own subtleties, complexities and cannot be easily adapted by an ordinary programmer. Thus, usability of our approach with integration to the Remix debugger has distinct advantages in building trusted smart contracts. Static analysis tools such as [25,27] are quite useful but have the limitations of static analysis of a dynamic language like Solidity. In fact, just like the undecidability of the access control problem (often called Harrison, Ruzzo and Ullman (HRU)), it can be shown that using the `delegatecall` etc., the "rights" of contracts will remain undecidable (we shall not go into details here). Hence, while static analysis approaches are useful in developing trusted programs as well as postmortem analysis, run time monitoring is preferable in our view where run-time checks cannot be avoided as we also need to keep in view the wallet/user smart contracts. As compared to systems like [24], ours is general and keeps to the debugging of a given contract rather than a general guideline and run time monitors are generated automatically.

Runtime verification approaches like [11], require specifications in exclusive specification languages like LARVA. Whereas our approach needs simple annotations from which one can generate the semantic preserving original contract keeping the annotations as constraints. This enables easy debugging of the contract and further provides a rough proof-outline gaining trust on the contract.

In summary, our run-time framework can be effectively used to overcome a spectrum of vulnerabilities through standard annotations and general annotations, as the run-time checks monitor the conditions on object state and enforce the synchronization requirements of smart contracts (cf. [4]).

8 Conclusions

In this paper, we have proposed a run-time framework for preventing some of the major vulnerabilities through simple intuitive programming annotations in Solidity contract through standard annotations from which the required run-time monitors can be generated automatically. It is also shown how the annotations described are similar in nature to that of declarative clauses in concurrent programming languages; the declarative clauses have been serving concerns of correctness as well as expressive power. Further, we have shown how the scope of the approach is quite expressive to include conditional contracts, contracts with overall constraints etc. Some of the main characteristics of our approach are:

1. For a large class of vulnerabilities, the run time monitors can be constructed automatically with standard annotations.
2. The approach of annotations is quite expressive. The INVAR clause can be effectively used for expressing a quite a lot of constraints as well as for constructing formal proofs; this class can also express some of the constraints expressed through ACCESS and PARALLEL.
3. The similarity of annotations with that declarative clauses also makes it possible to use those annotations in a modular way.
4. The transformation works at the Solidity level that preserves the original program structure and hence, debugging becomes natural.
5. As the run time monitors are on the blockchain, programmer gains confidence or trust on the contract even relative to his wallet contract and the run-time checks overcome false positives that are prevalent in static analysis methods and provides a rough proof-outline of the execution of the contract.

While we have illustrated similarity of standard annotations and declarations, we are working towards formal specification of the additional "declarative" structure needed in Solidity with a formal semantics. While the approach is definitely useful and extensible to different contexts, it would be nice to: (1) adapt the approach for proof carrying smart contracts [10] as that would really enhance the trust on the smart contract usage, (2) explore algorithms for elimination of run-time checks, and (3) optimize run-time checks to optimize the use of gas. It would be nice to have a constructive comparative evaluation of the various smart contract languages highlighted earlier to benefit smart contract programmers both qualitatively and quantitatively.

Acknowledgments. The work was carried out at the Centre of Excellence for Blockchains supported by Ripple Corporation. I wish to thank Snehal Borse, and Prateek Patidar who initially were responsible for building the basic prototype and to Hrishikesh Saloi and Mohammad Ummair, who have been re-engineering the system in Python to handle a spectrum vulnerabilities using this approach. Special thanks to Dr. Vishwas Patil of Center for Blockchain Research for his constructive comments on an initial draft of the paper.

References

1. Akentiev, A.: Parity multisig github. https://github.com/paritytech/parity/issues/6995
2. Amani, S., Bégel, M., Bortin, M., Staples, M.: Towards verifying Ethereum smart contract bytecode in Isabelle/HOL. In: Proceedings of the 7th ACM SIGPLAN International Conference on Certified Programs and Proofs, CPP 2018, pp. 66–77. ACM, New York (2018). https://doi.org/10.1145/3167084
3. Andrews, G.R., McGraw, J.R.: Language features for process interaction. SIGOPS Oper. Syst. Rev. 11(2), 114–127 (1977). https://doi.org/10.1145/390018.808318
4. Androulaki, E., et al.: Hyperledger fabric: a distributed operating system for permissioned blockchains. In: Proceedings of the Thirteenth EuroSys Conference, EuroSys 2018, pp. 30:1–30:15 (2018)
5. Atzei, N., Bartoletti, M., Cimoli, T.: A survey of attacks on Ethereum smart contracts (SoK). In: Maffei, M., Ryan, M. (eds.) POST 2017. LNCS, vol. 10204, pp. 164–186. Springer, Heidelberg (2017). https://doi.org/10.1007/978-3-662-54455-6_8
6. Bhargavan, K., et al.: Formal verification of smart contracts: short paper. In: Proceedings of the 2016 ACM Workshop on Programming Languages and Analysis for Security, PLAS 2016, pp. 91–96. ACM, New York (2016). https://doi.org/10.1145/2993600.2993611
7. Campbell, R.H., Habermann, A.N.: The specification of process synchronization by path expressions. In: Gelenbe, E., Kaiser, C. (eds.) OS 1974. LNCS, vol. 16, pp. 89–102. Springer, Heidelberg (1974). https://doi.org/10.1007/BFb0029355
8. Crafa, S., Di Pirro, M., Zucca, E.: Is solidity solid enough? In: Bracciali, A., Clark, J., Pintore, F., Rønne, P.B., Sala, M. (eds.) FC 2019. LNCS, vol. 11599, pp. 138–153. Springer, Cham (2020). https://doi.org/10.1007/978-3-030-43725-1_11
9. Das, A., Balzer, S., Hoffmann, J., Pfenning, F.: Resource-aware session types for digital contracts. CoRR abs/1902.06056 (2019)
10. Dickerson, T., Gazzillo, P., Herlihy, M., Saraph, V., Koskinen, E.: Proof-carrying smart contracts. In: Zohar, A., et al. (eds.) FC 2018. LNCS, vol. 10958, pp. 325–338. Springer, Heidelberg (2019). https://doi.org/10.1007/978-3-662-58820-8_22
11. Ellul, J., Pace, G.J.: Runtime verification of Ethereum smart contracts. In: 2018 14th European Dependable Computing Conference (EDCC), pp. 158–163 (2018). https://doi.org/10.1109/EDCC.2018.00036
12. Ethereum: Solidity documentation (2018). https://solidity.readthedocs.io/
13. Filliâtre, J.-C., Paskevich, A.: Why3—where programs meet provers. In: Felleisen, M., Gardner, P. (eds.) ESOP 2013. LNCS, vol. 7792, pp. 125–128. Springer, Heidelberg (2013). https://doi.org/10.1007/978-3-642-37036-6_8
14. Ghaleb, A., Pattabiraman, K.: How effective are smart contract analysis tools? Evaluating smart contract static analysis tools using bug injection. In: ISSTA 2020. Association for Computing Machinery, New York (2020). https://doi.org/10.1145/3395363.3397385
15. Grishchenko, I., Maffei, M., Schneidewind, C.: Foundations and tools for the static analysis of Ethereum smart contracts. In: Chockler, H., Weissenbacher, G. (eds.) CAV 2018. LNCS, vol. 10981, pp. 51–78. Springer, Cham (2018). https://doi.org/10.1007/978-3-319-96145-3_4
16. Grishchenko, I., Maffei, M., Schneidewind, C.: A semantic framework for the security analysis of Ethereum smart contracts. In: Bauer, L., Küsters, R. (eds.) POST 2018. LNCS, vol. 10804, pp. 243–269. Springer, Cham (2018). https://doi.org/10.1007/978-3-319-89722-6_10

17. Grossman, S., et al.: Online detection of effectively callback free objects with applications to smart contracts. **2**(POPL) (2017)
18. Guerraoui, R., Kuznetsov, P., Monti, M., Pavlovič, M., Seredinschi, D.A.: The consensus number of a cryptocurrency. In: Proceedings of the 2019 ACM Symposium on Principles of Distributed Computing, PODC 2019, pp. 307–316. Association for Computing Machinery, New York (2019)
19. Hansen, P.B., Dijkstra, E.W., Hoare, C.A.R.: The Origins of Concurrent Programming: From Semaphores to Remote Procedure Calls. Springer, Heidelberg (2002)
20. Hildenbrandt, E., et al.: KEVM: a complete formal semantics of the Ethereum virtual machine. In: 2018 IEEE 31st Computer Security Foundations Symposium (CSF), pp. 204–217 (2018)
21. Hirai, Y.: Defining the Ethereum virtual machine for interactive theorem provers. In: Brenner, M., et al. (eds.) FC 2017. LNCS, vol. 10323, pp. 520–535. Springer, Cham (2017). https://doi.org/10.1007/978-3-319-70278-0_33
22. Kolluri, A., Nikolic, I., Sergey, I., Hobor, A., Saxena, P.: Exploiting the laws of order in smart contracts. CoRR abs/1810.11605 (2018)
23. Krishna Rao, M.R.K., Kapur, D., Shyamasundar, R.K.: Proving termination of GHC programs. New Gen. Comput. **15**(3), 293–338 (1997). https://doi.org/10.1007/BF03037949
24. Lee, J.H.: DappGuard: active monitoring and defense for solidity smart contracts (2017)
25. Luu, L., Chu, D.H., Olickel, H., Saxena, P., Hobor, A.: Making smart contracts smarter. In: Proceedings of the 2016 ACM SIGSAC Conference on Computer and Communications Security, CCS 2016, pp. 254–269. ACM, New York (2016). https://doi.org/10.1145/2976749.2978309
26. Mueller(ConsenSys), B.: Mythril: a classic security analysis tool for Ethereum smart contracts (2017). https://github.com/ConsenSys/mythril
27. Nikolić, I., Kolluri, A., Sergey, I., Saxena, P., Hobor, A.: Finding the greedy, prodigal, and suicidal contracts at scale. In: Proceedings of the 34th Annual Computer Security Applications Conference, ACSAC 2018, pp. 653–663. Association for Computing Machinery, New York (2018)
28. Openzeppelin contributors: Safemath.sol (2019). https://github.com/OpenZeppelin/openzeppelin-solidity/blob/master/contracts/math/SafeMath.sol. Accessed 16 June 2019
29. Permenev, A., Dimitrov, D., Tsankov, P., Drachsler-Cohen, D., Vechev, M.: VerX: safety verification of smart contracts. In: 2020 IEEE Symposium on Security and Privacy (SP), pp. 414–430. Los Alamitos, CA, USA (2020)
30. Remix: Remix - Solidity IDE (2018). https://remix.ethereum.org/
31. Schneidewind, C., Grishchenko, I., Scherer, M., Maffei, M.: Ethor: practical and provably sound static analysis of Ethereum smart contracts (2020). https://doi.org/10.48550/ARXIV.2005.06227
32. Sergey, I., Hobor, A.: A concurrent perspective on smart contracts. In: Brenner, M., et al. (eds.) FC 2017. LNCS, vol. 10323, pp. 478–493. Springer, Cham (2017). https://doi.org/10.1007/978-3-319-70278-0_30
33. Shyamasundar, K.R.: A safety assessment of token standards for Ethereum: Erc20 and beyond. In: 6th Symposium on Distributed Ledger Technology (SDLT). SDLT, Gold Coast, Australia (2022)
34. Shyamsundar, R.K., Thatcher, J.W.: Language constructs for specifying concurrency in CDL. IEEE Trans. Softw. Eng. **15**(8), 977–993 (1989). https://doi.org/10.1109/32.31354

35. Tsankov, P., Dan, A., Drachsler-Cohen, D., Gervais, A., Bünzli, F., Vechev, M.: Securify: practical security analysis of smart contracts. In: Proceedings of the 2018 ACM SIGSAC Conference on Computer and Communications Security, CCS 2018, pp. 67–82. ACM, New York (2018). https://doi.org/10.1145/3243734.3243780
36. Zhang, W., Banescu, S., Pasos, L., Stewart, S., Ganesh, V.: MPRO: combining static and symbolic analysis for scalable testing of smart contract. arXiv abs/1911.00570 (2019)

Optimized Transaction Processing in Lightweight Distributed Ledger Networks for Internet of Things

Ali Tekeoglu[1]([✉])([iD]), Chen-Fu Chiang[2], Saumendra Sengupta[2],
Norman Noor Ahmed[3], Michael Stein[2], and Dilip Kusukuntla[2]

[1] Applied Physics Laboratory, Johns Hopkins University, Laurel, MD, USA
`ali.tekeoglu@jhuapl.edu`
[2] Computer Science Department, SUNY Polytechnic Institute, Utica, NY, USA
`{chiang,sengupta,steinm,kusukud}@sunypoly.edu`
[3] Air Force Research Laboratory/RIS, Rome, NY, USA
`norman.ahmed@us.af.mil`

Abstract. The last decade has witnessed proliferation of Internet of Things (IoT) devices ranging from smart-watches to smart-cities. Concurrently, first distributed ledger technology was introduced and gained significant traction. Blockchain, integrated into the IoT world presents variety of opportunities such as, machine-to-machine automated micro-transactions, trusted dissemination of information in trust-less network environments. There are many potential applications of blockchain technology in Smart City context, such as smart-homes, and smart-grid. However, the obstacles encountered when merging these two emerging technologies are many-fold. IoT devices are ubiquitous, but they have limited resources, while most popular blockchain technologies require a significant amount of computational resources to participate. Recently, there have been novel proposals which adopt lightweight distributed ledger technologies, that would let IoT devices to participate. One such ledger, IOTA's Tangle, uses a different underlying ledger data-structure, which is a directed-acyclic graph instead of a linked-list as in traditional blockchains. In this work, we have set-up a private, permissioned Tangle network, comprising of Raspberry-Pi devices as full-nodes and as transacting clients. Our previously proposed transaction optimization algorithm is implemented as an Nginx module.

Keywords: Blockchain · IoT · Tangle · TangoChain · Directed acyclic graph · Performance optimization

1 Introduction

Since the advent of Blockchain technology [1], it has been extensively applied in numerous fields, such as manufacturing, finance, medical, transportation, and

This work was supported by SFFP'20 program of Air Force Research Lab, under the supervision of Dr. Norman.

education. One of the major distinctive contributions from Blockchain is that it offers a time-stamped, ordered, decentralized and immutable distributed transaction ledger. Blockchain-based ledgers are tamper-proof from a single entity or a small collection of corrupted entities. The tamper-proof capability provides great interest and potential for the industry. This assumption is fair for smart city scenario.

One of the major drawbacks for Blockchain is the scalability issue. Take Bitcoin for example, the on-chain transaction processing capacity of the bitcoin network is limited by the average block creation time of 10 min and the original block size limit of 1 megabyte. These jointly constrain the network's throughput. The transaction processing capacity estimated using an average or median transaction size is between 3.3 and 7 transactions per second [2]. Similar Blockchain-based technologies, such as Ethereum, Algorand and Avalanche, have been improving the throughput performance issue. In addition, to dodge the performance bottleneck imposed by the Proof of Work (PoW) type of validation (consensus) in the Blockchain, many Blockchain-based technologies are shifting to Proof of Stake (PoS) in order to increase the throughput performance. The most noticeable case is Ethereum. It is in the process of transitioning its consensus mechanism from PoW to PoS, in an upgrade process known as "The Merge". The upgrade is performed by the Ethereum Foundation on September 15th according to Ethereum mainnet merge announcement. We list some of the pros and cons of PoW and PoS in Table 1 and Table 2 for comparison. Still, the improvement is far off from the performance of mainstream payment networks like Visa (2.4k transaction messages/s [3]).

Table 1. Pros and Cons of Proof-of-Work consensus mechanism

Pros	Cons
Prevents double-spending	Requires powerful mining hardware
Mining earns rewards	Prone to 51% attack
Random yet fair and more secure	Significant energy consumption

To address this scalability issue, researchers have endeavored in studies and practical deployments in limited IoT devices. These limited IoT devices are of limited capability in terms of computational power, memory and storage space. One of the notable architectures is IOTA [4], IoTeX, and WaltonChain. In the three aforementioned architecture, IOTA is the only one that uses its own Directed Acyclic Graph (DAG) based Blockchain, while the others use sub-chains connected through Ethereum Blockchain. Currently IOTA only supports PoW before IoTA 2.0. PoW or PoS in IOTA is not being used for consensus on double spends; IOTA uses Fast Probability Consensus (MANA), an augmented leaderless consensus mechanism to form consensus to solve the double spend problem, as well as an adaptive PoW which sets the difficulty higher for dishon-

Table 2. Pros and Cons of Proof-of-Stake consensus mechanism.

Pros	Cons
Safe from 51% of attacks	Double-spending are executable
Faster and inexpensive transactions	Control depends on capital
Low on energy consumption	Governance issues

est nodes. In essence making PoW the rate controller in order to solve the issue of spam attacks.

Conventional IoT devices generate and pass large quantity of data and transfer the data to a centralized server on the cloud for further use. The transfer to the cloud invokes concern over security and privacy and IoT devices have limited capability as aforementioned. Many of the IoT devices are battery-powered [5] and durability is another concern. To alleviate these inherent constraints from IoT devices, it is desirable to design Blockchains with a lightweight architecture.

In this paper, we present the current status of our ongoing foundational work towards a lightweight Directed Acyclic Graph (DAG) based distributed ledger infrastructure for resource constraint IoT devices in smart city context which we call it *TangoChain*. It's inspired by Tangle [4], and designed for a wide range of IoT application domains, especially geared towards smart city IoT devices. TangoChain is based on previously published [6–10] Tango algorithms and protocols that aims to improve the transaction synchronization and performance optimization of the Tangle blockchain. Thus, our contribution is the design and implementation of *TangoChain* prototype and the optimization protocols. We have organized the paper as follows; we first present related work in Sect. 2, followed by details of our system design and implementation. Conclusion and future work are discussed in Sect. 5.

2   Related Work

Tangle blockchain architecture has been adopted in various applications, such as vehicles [11], where the participating devices require low computation, and high performance. Investigation [5] showed that the computational overhead stays high for IoT devices. The computational overhead is the communication overhead to join the IOTA network. For the current stage of development, it is claimed that IOTA is not yet suitable for battery-powered IoT devices.

In the effort of reducing the storage requirement, a study [12] investigated the advantage of the Hypergraphs structure to release the pressure on data storage for IoT devices. It is through the partitions of Hypergraph-based blockchain network and the partitions are the hyperedges. Each hyperedge stores a part of transaction data. The study was implemented in a smart home network with several IoT devices. The storage performance is evaluated through simulations.

In structural health monitoring [13], studies investigated on integrating IoTs for transparent information sharing to automate decision making. Furthermore, the mechanism *sharding* was proposed to improve Blockchain's scalability [14] on the speed of transaction processing. In another study [15], a lightweight Blockchain architecture was proposed for smart-homes. This proposed architecture provides security and privacy using a distributed trust model. Such techniques reduce the block validation processing time with the hope of decreasing packet and processing overhead significantly. Other similar lightweight Blockchain management systems, such as Sensor-Chain [16], provided a superior reduction in resource consumption. This architecture aims to address the scalability issue around data collection, storage, and analytics for Cyber Physical Systems (CPS).

3 System Design and Implementation

3.1 Graph Theoretical Description of Tango's DAG

Tango is a Directed Acyclic Graph designed as an extension based on original Tangle [4] that is used for IOTA networks. Tango is represented as a graph $T = (V, E)$, where V is the set of vertices (i.e.; transactions) and E is the set of directed edges (i.e.; approval/confirmation). The incoming and outgoing degrees of a node $v \in V$ is define as follows:

$$deg_{in}(v) = |\{e = (u, v) \in E\}| \tag{1}$$
$$deg_{out}(v) = |\{e = (v, u) \in E\}|. \tag{2}$$

For $u, v \in V$, we say that u approves v, if $(u, v) \in E$. If $deg_{in}(w) = 0$ (i.e.; there are no edges pointing to w), then we say that $w \in V$ is a transaction in process (tip), which also means there is no other transaction that approves w yet. The first vertex, $\alpha \in V$, in the DAG is the genesis such that $deg_{out}(\alpha) = 0$. It is thus clear that $\forall v \in V, v \neq \alpha$, there exists a directed path from v to α.

3.2 PITEC Model Basics

In our previous efforts, we designed several protocols for Tango on top of Tangle's DAG based blockchain, to improve system performance and crucial system properties such as; scalability, decentralization, synchronicity and efficient diffusion of new transactions amongst network participants. In order to achieve more synchronous transaction processing we proposed "Decentralized Semi-Synchronous Pulse Diffusion" (DSPD) protocol [9]. In addition, "Pulsed Injection of Transactions into the Evaluation Corridor" (PITEC) protocol was designed to queue up the un-evaluated transactions at controllers and inject them to evaluators/verifiers in a harmonious way with periodic cycles [9]. These protocols aimed at optimizing overall network performance for transaction processing and information dissemination. Further improvements to DSPD and PITEC we introduced in [6–8,10]

The aim of PITEC is to regulate the amount of transactions released into the system to minimize the cost per cycle. Let A be a constant cost per cycle, which is proportional to the number of transactions released into the system for a given cycle. In the original work, c_f is the unit cost per such transaction per cycle. It then requires $v \propto \rho c_f n_t$, where ρ is a suitable constant, and v is the cost per such transaction per unit time. Let n_t and $\hat{n}_t$ be the actual and estimated number of transactions that would not make the verification in the cycle index t as because they were faulty, or were not visible, and hence, did not get picked.

Ideally, they should be zero in every cycle in which case the optimal number of the fresh transaction appearing for verification at the beginning of every new cycle should be infinitely large. To compute n_t for the next cycle t, we need to formulate it via some simple estimation routine.

Initially $n_0 = \widehat{n_0}$ as the initial estimate, and the iterative estimation procedure is as below

$$\hat{n}_t = max(\zeta, \alpha_t \times n_{t-1} + (1 - \alpha_t) \times \widehat{n_{t-1}}) \qquad (3)$$

where ζ is some constant, α is the smoothing factor where $0 < \alpha < 1.0$. The average transaction latency cost v per transaction per unit time in a given cycle is $v \propto \rho c_f \hat{n}_t$. Since ρ is a constant, we can simply assume that $v \propto c_f \hat{n}_t$. To make it a realistic computation, it is necessary to include the possibility that sometimes in a cycle we may not get any faulty or ignored transactions. In that case, previous cycle estimate would be a good choice to stick to.

The cost of the total cost per unit time to is minimized at the t_{th} cycle is thus

$$C_t = \frac{A}{T_t} + \frac{n_t v_t}{2}. \qquad (4)$$

where A is the constant set up cost and it should remain constant for all cycles. If the transactions are consumed (affixed) at a rate of D_t transactions per unit time, $n_t = D_t T_t$, and then we obtain

$$C_t = \frac{A D_t}{n_t} + \frac{1}{2} n_t v_t \qquad (5)$$

This leads to an optimum pulse injection size of n_t^* that

$$n_t^* = \sqrt{\frac{2 A D_t}{v_t}} \quad where \quad T_t = \sqrt{\frac{2A}{v_t D_t}} \qquad (6)$$

as the corresponding cycle time is defined as T_t in above Eq. (6). This is a basic EOQ (Economic Order Quantity) model often used in buffer management and inventory control problems.

3.3 Formulas to be Used in Future Physical Experimental Setup

We will associate the cost in terms of CPU usage for A and v. Let us choose the learning rate to be α_{init}. Let there be two systems, X and Y. System X is the configuration of Tangle without PITEC protocol while Y is adapts PITEC. We need to rewrite the formula as follows. We need to use prior knowledge to predict as shown in Eq. 3. The cost of the total cost per unit time in i-th cycle of T_t units of time is given in Eq. 4. In reality, at each cycle we do not know exactly the average latency cost v_t nor the consumption rate D_t at cycle i till the cycle i is over. We can approximate and recalibrate using smoothing factors. At the end of cycle $t-1$, we have the information regarding the actual v_{t-1} and D_{t-1}. Since $\widehat{v_t}, \widehat{D_t}$ are predictions based on the previous cycle, we do

$$\widehat{v_t} = (\beta_t \times v_{t-1} + (1 - \beta_t) \times \widehat{v_{t-1}})$$
$$\widehat{D_t} = (\gamma_t \times D_{i-1} + (1 - \gamma_t) \times \widehat{D_{i-1}}) \tag{7}$$

where $0 < \beta, \gamma < 1$ as smoothing factors for prediction functions for v_t and D_t.
    This leads to an optimum pulse injection size of n_t^* that

$$n_t^* = \sqrt{\frac{2 A \widehat{D_i}}{\widehat{v_i}}} \quad \text{where} \quad T_t = \sqrt{\frac{2A}{\widehat{v_i} \widehat{D_i}}}. \tag{8}$$

    For a more dynamic system, we can make our smooth factors more adaptive. At the beginning of t_{th} cycle, we approximate to get $\widehat{n_t}, \widehat{v_t}$ and $\widehat{D_t}$ using Eq. 7 and Eq. 3. At the end of the $t_t h$ cycle, we have the real values for n_t, v_t and D_t. Let the ratios be

$$r_t^\alpha = \frac{n_t}{\widehat{n_t}}, \quad r_t^\beta = \frac{v_t}{\widehat{v_t}}, \quad r_t^\gamma = \frac{D_t}{\widehat{D_t}}. \tag{9}$$

    For the $(t+1)_{th}$ cycle, if the ratio is greater than a threshold, δ_{up}, or smaller than a threshold δ_{dn}, one adjusts the smoothing factor accordingly. For the large ratio case, we set

$$\Delta_{t+1} = \min\{1, \Delta t + \frac{r_t^\Delta - \delta_{up}}{2 * r_t^\Delta}(1 - \Delta_t)\} \tag{10}$$

and in a small ratio case (prediction way higher than the reality), we need to lower the coefficient of prediction, eg. $(1 - \alpha_t)\widehat{n_t}$, we set

$$\Delta_{t+1} = \min\{1, \Delta t + (\frac{\delta_{dn} - r_t^\Delta}{2 * \delta_{dn}})(1 - \Delta_t)\} \tag{11}$$

where $\Delta_t \in \{\alpha_t, \beta_t, \gamma_t\}$.
    Figure 1 depicts the parameters used and the way they are calculated in our physical network, adapted from PITEC protocol (Table 3).

Table 3. Variables in formulas and their definitions where the consumption rate is in terms of number of transactions per unit time whereas the carry over cost is how long the transaction remaining pending (unfixed) + that transaction's amount in the ledger system .

Variable	Definition
n_t	Actual injection quantity at the t_{th} cycle
n_t^*	Predicted injection quantity at the t_{th} cycle
T_t	Duration (time) of the t_{th} cycle
D_t	Consumption rate at the t_{th} cycle
v_t	Carry-over cost for the t_{th} cycle

D = # of transactions per unit time (tps)
T = cycle time (seconds)
A = constant **cost** per cycle (i.e. *avg cpu usage of hornet process*)
v = The transaction carrying **cost** v per transaction per unit time in a given cycle

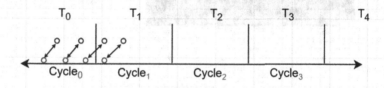

- Start monitoring transactions at T=0 seconds
- Calculate Q_1^* based on the the number of transactions processed in Cycle0 divided by Cycle0 time (seconds) = D

Fig. 1. PITEC protocol parameters explained

4 Proposed Future Work

4.1 Network Implementation

Physical test-bed implementation started with a private network that runs Go version of IOTA's Tangle Blockchain. A private Tangle is an IOTA network that you control and that contains only nodes that you know. A private Tangle uses the same technology as the public IOTA networks, except you control it by running an open-source implementation of the Coordinator called Compass. You can use Compass to allow nodes in your own IOTA network to reach a consensus on Compass' milestones instead of the Coordinator's ones.

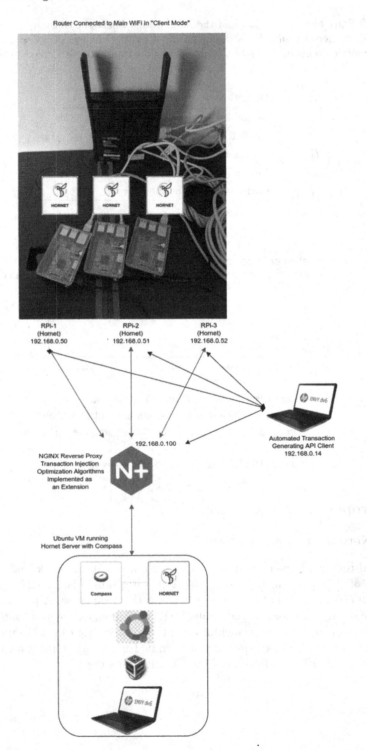

Fig. 2. RPI-3B's connected to LAN and will run Hornets w/o Compass

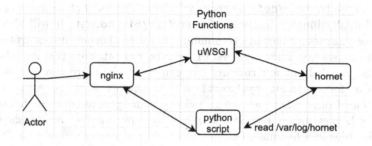

Fig. 3. Two approaches to implement our transaction optimization algorithm PITEC behind NginX

Our network implementation is depicted in Fig. 2. In this private Tangle setup, we have 3 raspberry-pis running Hornet (Go implementation of IOTA Tangle). One of the Hornet is acting as coordinator, by running the Compass plugin on top of Hornet. This node is running in an Ubuntu VM on a laptop.

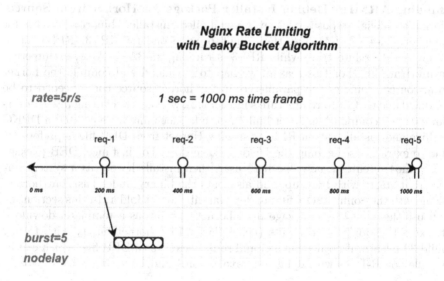

Fig. 4. Original NginX request queuing model

Setting up Main Hornet Node with Compass. We used an Ubuntu virtual machine inside VirtualBox on a laptop to act as the main Hornet node in the private tangle. This VM's specifications are better than the R-Pis, since it is supposed to run the Compass plug-in on top of Hornet. Since Hornet has an Ubuntu repository, installation is quite straightforward; Following commands will install Hornet on Ubuntu; `sudo apt-get update`; `sudo apt-get install hornet`. After installation, *config* files are located under `/var/lib/hornet`, a default file under `/etc/default/hornet` where additional cli arguments can be set, and finally binary Hornet file under `/usr/bin/hornet`. It will also create a new user `hornet`. Following command will enable hornet auto-starts at boot and run as a service. `sudo systemctl enable hornet.service`. At this point, hornet is installed but not running. We can check the current status of hornet daemon as follows, `sudo systemctl status hornet.service` And also read the log files from hornet daemon as follows; `sudo journalctl -u hornet -f`, where -*u* hornet means the hornet unit is systemd, and -*f* means show most recent log files in a live manner.

Setting up Raspberry-Pis. We are planning to use 3 Raspberry-Pi-3B (Rpi3) v1.2 (from 2015)[1] in our experiments as hornet nodes. They didn't have the Compass plugin, only the Ubuntu virtual machine running in Virtualbox had the Compass as the Tangle network Coordinator. The main reason to use Raspberry-Pi3B was to show that this blockchain architecture is feasible for resource limited IoT devices, such as devices commonly deployed in a smart city application. Hardware specs for the RPI versions we have used is provided in the Table 4.

Building ARMHF Debian Installer Package for Hornet from Source. Hornet's official repository has pre-compiled installer binaries (.deb) for RaspberryPi-4 (RPI-4), but they don't provide one for RPI-3. RPI-4 has a 64-bit ARM architecture, while RPI-3 is running on 32-bit ARM architecture (armv7l/armhf). For this reason, we had to download and compile the hornet from source. Some of the parameters in the hornet source code, needed to be modified due to 32 bit architecture's integer size, which were causing integer overflows during compilation. After building the hornet binary, we created a DPKG archive and installed it on RPIs. Installing Hornet from DEB file is preferable, due to extra house-keeping the DEB package does. For instance, DEB package (for arm64) creates a new "hornet" user, then installs hornet as a system service that starts with boot-up, and also puts the binary under /usr/bin/hornet, along with the config JSON files under /var/lib/hornet folder. In this section, we will use the arm64 deb package from hornet's github as a template, download it, extract, modify the contents (i.e. replace 64-bit hornet binary with freshly build 32-bit armhf hornet binary) and re-package it as a DEB file, which can be installed on R-Pi-3s with `dpkg --install` command.

NginX as a Reverse Proxy. Proxying is typically used to distribute the load among several servers. In this case, we install Nginx as Reverse Proxy on the same machine as a Hornet node that has Compass as seen in Fig. 2. Even if there is only one node in the network, deployment of a reverse proxy right in front of the node is considered to be safer, and recommended as a best practice. Adding a reverse proxy, provides an additional security layer that enables IP address filtering, bandwidth rate limiting, SSL encrypting, additional authorization layer and load balancing, to name a few.

---

[1] https://www.raspberrypi.org/products/raspberry-pi-3-model-b/.

Table 4. Hardware and Software Specification for each machine that will be used in the experiments

Device	Ubuntu VM	Raspberry-Pi 3B+
Operating system	Ubuntu 18.04.5 LTS	Raspbian Buster 10
Memory	2 GB	1 GB
Disk space	50 GB	15 GB
CPU	x86 (64bits)	armv7l (32bits)
Hornet	v1.0.1	v1.0.1

The original NginX queuing algorithm is Leaky Bucket. Which is detailed in Fig. 4.

Figure 3 shows two different approaches to implement transaction optimization algorithm, PITEC protocol.

5 Conclusion

We have designed an architecture to test and implement the PISTIS protocol integration into IOTA/Tangle to optimize the transaction processing. We are working on the implementation of the protocol as an Nginx plugin in a future work.

References

1. Nakamoto, S.: Bitcoin: a peer-to-peer electronic cash system (2008). https://bitcoin.org/bitcoin.pdf
2. Croman, K., et al.: On scaling decentralized blockchains. In: Clark, J., Meiklejohn, S., Ryan, P.Y.A., Wallach, D., Brenner, M., Rohloff, K. (eds.) FC 2016. LNCS, vol. 9604, pp. 106–125. Springer, Heidelberg (2016). https://doi.org/10.1007/978-3-662-53357-4_8
3. https://usa.visa.com/dam/VCOM/download/corporate/media/visanet-technology/visa-net-booklet.pdf
4. Popov, S.: The Tangle. IOTA Foundation, Strassburgerstraße 55, 10405 Berlin Germany, Technical report, version 1.4.3, 30 April 2018. https://tinyurl.com/y55h5w2n
5. Elsts, A., Mitskas, E., Oikonomou, G.: Distributed ledger technology and the internet of things: a feasibility study. In: Proceedings of the 1st Workshop on Blockchain-enabled Networked Sensor Systems, Seriex BlockSys 2018, pp. 7–12. ACM, New York (2018). https://tinyurl.com/y55xr9qt
6. Andriamanalimanana, B., Chiang, C.-F., Novillo, J., Sengupta, S., Tekeoglu, A.: Parameterized pulsed transaction injection computation model and performance optimizer for IOTA-tango. In: Xhafa, F., Leu, F.-Y., Ficco, M., Yang, C.-T. (eds.) 3PGCIC 2018. LNDECT, vol. 24, pp. 74–84. Springer, Cham (2019). https://doi.org/10.1007/978-3-030-02607-3_7

7. Andriamanalimanana, B., Chiang, C.-F., Novillo, J., Sengupta, S., Tekeoglu, A.: Semi-synchronocity enabling protocol and pulsed injection protocol for a distributed ledger system. In: Xhafa, F., Leu, F.-Y., Ficco, M., Yang, C.-T. (eds.) 3PGCIC 2018. LNDECT, vol. 24, pp. 26–35. Springer, Cham (2019). https://doi.org/10.1007/978-3-030-02607-3_3

8. Andriamanalimanana, B., Chiang, C., Novillo, J., Sengupta, S., Tekeoglu, A.: A probabilistic model of periodic pulsed transaction injection. In: 2018 2nd Cyber Security in Networking Conference (CSNet), pp. 1–5 (2018)

9. Andriamanalimanana, B., Chiang, C., Novillo, J., Sengupta, S., Tekeoglu, A.: Tango: the beginning-a semi-synchronous Iota-Tangle type distributed ledger with periodic pulsed entries. In: 2018 2nd Cyber Security in Networking Conference (CSNet) (2018)

10. Sengupta, S., Chiang, C.-F., Andriamanalimanana, B., Novillo, J., Tekeoglu, A.: A hybrid adaptive transaction injection protocol and its optimization for verification-based decentralized system. Future Internet **11**(8) (2019). https://www.mdpi.com/1999-5903/11/8/167

11. Rathore, H., Samant, A., Jadliwala, M.: TangleCV: a distributed ledger technique for secure message sharing in connected vehicles. ACM Trans. Cyber-Phys. Syst. **5**(1), 1–25 (2021). https://doi.org/10.1145/3404500

12. Qu, C., Tao, M., Yuan, R.: A hypergraph-based blockchain model and application in internet of things-enabled smart homes. Sensors **18**(9), 2784 (2018)

13. Jo, B.W., Khan, R.M.A., Lee, Y.-S.: Hybrid blockchain and internet-of-things network for underground structure health monitoring. Sensors **18**(12) (2018). https://www.mdpi.com/1424-8220/18/12/4268

14. Chow, S.S.M., Lai, Z., Liu, C., Lo, E., Zhao, Y.: Sharding blockchain. In: 2018 IEEE International Conference on Blockchain, p. 1665 (2018)

15. Dorri, A., Kanhere, S.S., Jurdak, R.: Towards an optimized blockchain for IoT. In: 2017 IEEE/ACM Second International Conference on Internet-of-Things Design and Implementation (IoTDI), pp. 173–178 (2017)

16. Shahid, A., Pissinou, N., Staier, C., Kwan, R.: Sensor-chain: a lightweight scalable blockchain framework for internet of things. In: 2019 IEEE International Conference Blockchain (2019)

Short Paper Track

Shackled: A 3D Rendering Engine Programmed Entirely in Ethereum Smart Contracts

Ike[(✉)] and BarefootDev

Spectra, Perth, Australia
{ike,barefootdev}@spectra.art
http://www.spectra.art/

Abstract. The Ethereum blockchain permits the development and deployment of smart contracts which can store and execute code "on-chain" — that is, entirely on nodes in the blockchain's network. Smart contracts have traditionally been used for financial purposes, but since smart contracts are Turing-complete, their algorithmic scope is broader than any single domain. To that end, we design, develop, and deploy a comprehensive 3D rendering engine programmed entirely in Ethereum smart contracts, called Shackled. Shackled computes a 2D image from a 3D scene, executing every single computation on-chain, on Ethereum. To our knowledge, Shackled is the first and only fully on-chain 3D rendering engine for Ethereum. In this work, we 1) provide three unique datasets for the purpose of using and benchmarking Shackled, 2) execute said benchmarks and provide results, 3) demonstrate a potential use case of Shackled in the domain of tokenised generative art, 4) provide a no-code user interface to Shackled, 5) enumerate the challenges associated with programming complex algorithms in Solidity smart contracts, and 6) outline potential directions for improving the Shackled platform. It is our hope that this work increases the Ethereum blockchain's native graphics processing capabilities, and that it enables increased use of smart contracts for more complex algorithms, thus increasing the overall richness of the Ethereum ecosystem.

Keywords: 3D rendering · Rendering engine · Blinn-Phong lighting · On-chain · Ethereum · Blockchain · Smart contracts · Solidity · Non-fungible tokens · NFTs

1 Introduction

The Ethereum blockchain has often been described as a "World Computer" [B+] as it offers a smart contract platform that allows for general algorithms to be ran

---

Ike and BarefootDev—The work detailed in this paper was completed online via contributions from pseudonymous collaborators "on-chain" — that is, entirely on nodes in the blockchain's network. Smart contract code has interesting and novel benefits [ZXD+20], namely; immutability (records on Ethereum cannot be edited once committed to a block), permanance (the code lasts as long as the blockchain remains in existence), transparency (all smart contract source code is visible publically), scalability (smart contract code can be executed on any node in the network), exact reproducibility (other programs can execute the code identically given the same inputs), and composability (other programs can use the code as a building block in a larger system).

In this work, we program a 3D rendering engine — that is, a program which takes as input a three dimensional scene, and computes as an output a two dimensional image representing what that scene would look like from a given camera pose — entirely within Solidity smart contracts. We then deploy it on the Ethereum blockchain. We name the engine *Shackled* due to its on-*chain* nature. To the best of our knowledge, **Shackled is the first fully on-chain 3D rendering engine**.

The contributions of this work are as follows:

1. Quantification of the efficiency of Shackled in terms of gas usage.
2. *Three* 3D object datasets that are compatible with Shackled.
3. A demonstration of the utility of Shackled: we develop and deploy a generative art project (*Shackled Genesis*), integrating Shackled with non-fungible tokens (NFTs).
4. A user interface to the Shackled smart contract library called *Shackled Creator*[1], which allows users to render 3D objects entirely on the blockchain through a simple, no-code, visual interface on the web.
5. A complete discussion regarding the challenges of programming complex algorithms as Solidity smart contracts.

2   Related Work

Solidity smart contracts are a relatively young technology [Dan17], and have been used for primarily financial use cases. Perhaps most notably, enabling the development of Decentralised Finance (DeFi); a class of finance characterised by blockchain-based trustlessness and secure peer-to-peer transactions in the absence of a trusted third party [CPP21]. However, the applications of smart contracts extend well beyond the domain of finance, with on-chain implementations of complex algorithms appearing in the Ethereum ecosystem (e.g., an on-chain chess engine [fiv21]).

One novel yet controversial application of smart contracts is the **tokenisation of art** NFTs [WLWC21,Cho21]. NFTs have been criticised for their implications on traditional copyright law [Gol21], breaches of intellectual property [Yod22], effect on art [Fry21], environmental impact [TBDI22] (this is discussed in the context in this project in Appendix A), over-hyped status in the modern

---

[1] Available at https://shackled.spectra.art/#/creator.

in zeitgeist [MB21], and their lack of regulation promoting a predatory culture of scamming, manipulation, and fraud [TM20].

Conversely, they have also been praised for redefining the nature of ownership in the digital age [WLWC21, Cho21], status as a novel investment opportunity, and for the *positive* effect that they have had on art culture [Kug21] and collectorship.

Much work has been done regarding the tokenisation of art, including Ethereum-based generative art projects [Hub21, HA21, Nou21], on-chain graphics libraries [Wu21], storing of 3D objects on-chain [say22], and using on-chain technology for the generation and preservation of digital art [MJ19, MJ17, Hol22].

At the intersection of art tokenisation and smart contract programming is the potential for performing **3D rendering** on-chain. Approaches to decentralised 3D rendering are being explored and commercialised [Tok17], with a focus on large-scale computing on custom blockchains by leveraging graphs of computing nodes [Alc22, WJL+20] optimised for graphics processing. These approaches transfer the hardware burden from the user to a decentralised network of compute providers, essentially creating a market for specialised computation.

Although Solidity smart contracts represent a great opportunity for algorithmic development, the scale of computation that they allow at this time is limited; modern graphics engines could not currently be implemented in Solidity. As such, Shackled is based on the work of early graphics pioneers, using technology from nearly 50 years ago (which is more suited for implementation on-chain today). Specifically, we modify versions of Bui Tong Phuong's [Pho75] and Jim Blinn's [Bli77] original 3D rendering and lighting models, and use them to create a Solidity version of a simple rendering pipeline inspired by OpenGL [SA99].

3   Datasets

We begin by developing and presenting three datasets in Table 1 for use with Shackled which will be used throughout this work (see Appendix B for data availability). Firstly, the **Shackled Genesis Dataset**, which comprises 1024 triangular prism-based geometries generated using an on-chain geometry generating algorithm. Secondly, the **Shackled Icons Dataset**, which is comprised of a series of hand-crafted 3D objects. Thirdly, the **Shackled Common Graphics Objects Dataset**, which is comprised of common objects from 3D graphics history, processed for compatability with Shackled.

4   Approach

4.1   Development

Shackled was developed using common development tools for programming and testing Solidity smart contracts on Ethereum. Our **technical stack** included *Hardhat* as the primary development environment, *Ethers* for interfacing with the smart contracts, and *Chai* for testing. We catalogue the development challenges and how they were overcome in Table 1.

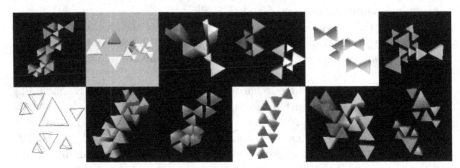

(a) Examples from the **Shackled Genesis Dataset**, as rendered in Shackled. Each instance features a number of triangular prisms placed generatively and rendered with different colour and lighting parameters. There are 1024 instances in the dataset.

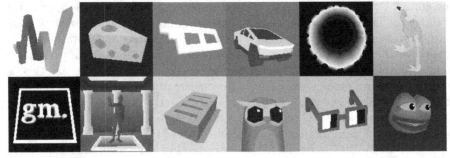

(b) Examples from the **Shackled Icons Dataset**, as rendered in Shackled. The subjects of each render were chosen for recognisability and relevance in the on-chain art and NFT community.

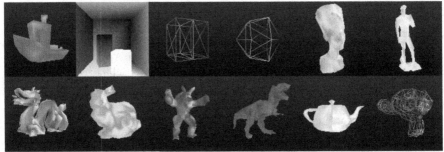

(c) Examples from the **Shackled Common Graphics Object Dataset**, as rendered in Shackled. **Top row**: 3DBenchy (3D printing benchmark), Cornell's box [GTGB84], wireframe renders of a Cube and an Isosphere, a 3D scan of the bust of Nefertiti [WB82], and a 3D scan of Michaelangelo's sculpture David [LPC+00]. **Bottom row**: Stanford's Dragon, Bunny, Armadillo, and Tyra [Sta14], the Utah Teapot, and Blender's Suzanne [Bla19].

Fig. 1. Datasets used in this work.

Table 1. Descriptions of development challenges and the solutions used to overcome them during the development of Shackled. We categorise the challenges as being imposed by Solidity, or by the Ethereum ecosystem.

Description	Solution
Solidity programming language challenges	
No support for floating point or fixed-point numbers	Use whole numbers in the gwei designation (10^9)
Data types less than 32 bytes being assembled into the same storage slot, reducing division precision	Pad variables to ensure they take up 32 bytes, and use unit tests to ensure correct behavior
Overflow and underflow errors are common as integers are a fixed size	The latest versions of Solidity include automatic checks for these errors
Limited best-practice documentation	Learn from exemplar projects (all on-chain code is open source)
Uninformative stack trace errors	use development environments such as Hardhat
Limited/no typecasting	Develop workarounds for types that can't be cast to other types. There is not necessarily a 'catch-all' solution to this issue
Only 16 variables being usable at a time due to the stack depth limit	Use structs to store and pass variables
Ethereum ecosystem challenges	
Exceeding gas limits imposed by node providers	Run your own node or find a provider willing to provide a higher limit (Alchemy in our case)
Modifying/writing storage incurs significant expense on the Ethereum blockchain	No general solution, but on-chain compression and generation can be useful to avoid directly storing data
True randomness is not possible as Ethereum is deterministic	Psuedorandomness can be achieved by using a block's hash or number as input
The EVM stack has only 1024 slots available for functions calling other functions	Use loops in lieu of recursion

To benchmark Shackled and **estimate the cost of computation**, we estimate the amount of **gas**; a unit describing the amount of computational power required to perform some specific computation on the Ethereum network [B+]. Our gas estimation approach involves binary searching the upper and lower gas limits until a 'not enough gas' error is triggered; we repeatedly attempt to complete renders with less and less gas until we converge on the true gas required to perform a specific render operation, allowing us to accurately measure the computational cost of completing a given render.

Importantly, Shackled does not require the expenditure of gas to perform rendering operations. The entire rendering operation is implemented in a *read call*, and thus does not *write* any data to the Ethereum blockchain. **As such, all gas estimations presented in this study are *gas-equivalents*,** e.g., a Shackled render benchmarked at 10 billion units of gas does not actually consume that amount of gas, but its computational cost is equivalent to an operation that would consume that amount.

4.2   Design of the Rendering Pipeline

Shackled converts a 3D model into a 2D image using a sequential rendering pipeline inspired by OpenGL [SA99] and modified for on-chain implementation and execution (see Fig. 2). The key steps are as follows.

Vertex specification involves providing the 3D positions and colours for all points in the object's mesh. Faces will be constructed from these 3-vectors as per the .obj file format specification [MB08].

The **vertex shader** is traditionally a program written in a language designed for accelerated computation on graphics hardware, which allows for parallel processing of independent vertex computations. In Shackled, we have no such accelerative capability. The vertex shader still assumes the traditional role of projecting the points using a perspective or orthographic camera matrix, and transforming the points via a model view matrix (translations and scaling are supported), converting the points to world space.

Fig. 2. The results of the key steps of the Shackled rendering pipeline for rending a single triangle. **From left to right**, we display the outputs of 1) vertex specification, 2) the vertex shader, 3) primitive assembly, 4) rasterization, 5) the fragment shader, 6) compositing and image buffer return. Ultimately the render comprises of a red-green-blue coloured triangle light with a harsh specular light with a steep fall-off from the bottom right, composited onto a blue gradient background. All steps are computed on the Ethereum blockchain entirely within smart contracts. (Color figure online)

Primitive assembly involves taking groups of 3 vertices and constructing triangles out of them (Shackled only supports triangulated objects as input). The vertex indices of the triangles are specified during vertex specification. No form of clipping or frustrum culling is performed at this stage.

Rasterization uses a combination of Bresenham's algorithm [Koo87] and the Scanline algorithm [LC79] to convert sets of three vertices into a wireframe triangle, and then into a filled triangle with interpolated colours. No form of anti-aliasing or subpixel interpolation is implemented. Fragments (candidate pixels) may overlap at this stage (i.e., have the same (x, y) position in the final image), but will be discarded if they are outside of the bounds of the canvas.

The **fragment shader** applies Blinn-Phong shading [Pho75, Bli77] to each fragment depending on the lighting configuration provided. The projected depths of each fragment are also used for depth testing, and only the closest fragments are kept (i.e., near parts of the object are rendered in favor of far away parts of the object if they occupy the same position in the render).

Compositing is the process whereby the pixel data is written into an image buffer (i.e. a 2D matrix with an RGB tuple at each element), and applied on top of a background. Shackled supports the generation of unicolour backgrounds, or two-color vertical gradient backgrounds. The image buffer is then encoded as a bitmap image.

4.3   Deployment

Shackled's on-chain code consists of 13 smart contracts and libraries. The deployment of Shackled cost $0.258\varXi$ (427 USD at the time) and the deployment of Shackled Icons (a follow up tokenised art collection) cost $0.05\varXi$ (80 USD at the time). The cost of the follow up project was significantly less as the rendering engine code had already been deployed and could be used in a composable manner. The deployed and verified contracts can be found in Appendix B. These projects tokenised the renders of Shackled as ERC-721A tokens (i.e., NFTs), demonstrating Shackled's commercial potential and viability in niche rendering use cases.

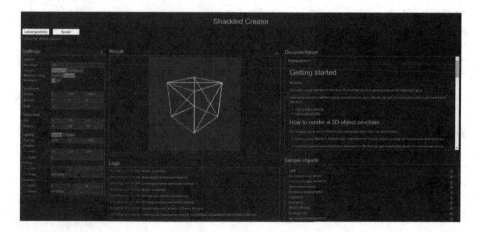

Fig. 3. Shackled *Creator*; a simple user interface to the Shackled rendering engine contracts. Note that rotation is provided as a transformation, however, the rotation matrix multiplications are calculated off-chain in the front-end. All other computations are performed on-chain.

We also implemented, deployed, and provided a custom **user interface** (UI) to the Shackled smart contracts which enables a user to use Shackled for on-chain 3D rendering without any expertise in on-chain programming, Solidity, or smart contracts (see Fig. 3). This UI — Shackled *Creator* — is free to use and publically available[2].

5   Results and Discussion

5.1   Computation Scales Quadratically with Canvas Size

We render the same object from a canvas size of 8×8 to 128×128 doubling the canvas size in each axis for each step. We use our gas estimation procedure to estimate the computational cost, and plot it in Fig. 4 (right). We compute two sets of results: one using the perspective camera projection model, and one using the orthographic camera projection model. The resultant renders are depicted in Fig. 4 (left).

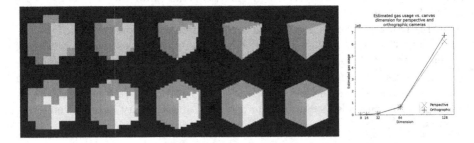

Fig. 4. Rendering different cubes on-chain whilst varying canvas size and camera model parameters. **Left, top row**: varying the canvas size from 8–128 pixels using a perspective camera. **Left, bottom row**: varying the canvas size from 8–128 pixels using an orthographic camera. **Right**: plotting the gas estimates as a function of canvas size for each render using the perspective and orthographic camera settings.

We note that the computation cost scales quadratically with the canvas size, as expected due to the quadratic increase in fragments with canvas size. Additionally, the computation cost is invariant to the camera projection model. This quadratic scaling greatly limits the scalability of Shackled to larger renders, and potential improvements to alleviate this issue are suggested in Sect. 6.

---

[2] Available at https://shackled.spectra.art/#/creator.

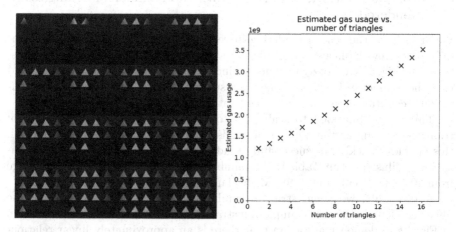

Fig. 5. Left: the resultant renders from testing how the gas cost scales with the number of rendered pixels. The gas-pixel relationship is explored by rendering 1–16 identical triangles, which result in a near-identical number of pixels per triangle in the final render. **Right:** the estimated gas usage increases approximately linearly with the number of triangles, and thus pixels. We note that the y-axis offset suggests that there is a constant amount of gas which is always 'paid' regardless of the render.

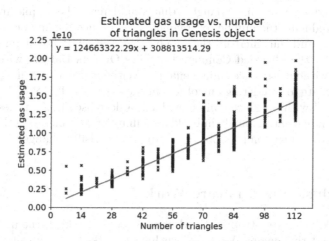

Fig. 6. Estimated gas costs plotted against number of triangles in the rendered object, for every instance of the Shackled Genesis Dataset (see Table 1). A linear fit is applied using the NumPy package's *polyfit* function [HMvdW+20], and the result is plotted and displayed. Each triangular prism in each instance is comprised of 7 triangles: 1 for the front face, and 2 triangles each for the 3 sides of the prism (the prisms have no back), hence the 7 unit separation in the x-axis.

5.2   Computation Scales Linearly with the Number of Triangles Rendered

We investigate the cost of rendering increasing numbers of pixels by incrementally rendering duplicates of an identical geometry (a single triangle), as illustrated in Fig. 5. We note that linearly increasing the number of triangles (and thus the number of fragments/pixels), results in a linear increase in the computational cost (as approximated by estimated gas).

This allows Shackled to scale well to geometries with a large number of triangles, as long as the number of pixels on screen remains bounded. Indeed, this enables Shackled to successfully render an expressive range of objects on-chain, as illustrated in Table 1; the number of triangles in these objects range from 20 (default cube) to 1198 (Michaelangelo's David).

Additionally, we demonstrate a similar pattern using the entirety of the Shackled Genesis Dataset (samples illustrated in Table 1). The results are shown in Fig. 6 and demonstrate again that there is an approximately linear relationship between the number of rendered pixels and the cost of computation (again approximated by estimated gas).

5.3   Backface Culling Reduces Computation Significantly

Furthermore, we investigate how backface culling [Bli93] — an approach which analyses the normal vector of a triangle as it compares to the direction that the camera is pointing — can greatly reduce the number of fragments that are computed by removing triangles that would never be visible in the final render. By reducing the number of fragments, we reduce the amount of required computation, and thus increase the capability of the rendering engine.

We render the Shackled Common Graphics Objects Dataset with backface culling and without backface culling enabled. Without backface culling, the average gas estimate for rendering any object in the dataset is 1.54×10^{11}, compared to 4.39×10^{10} with backface culling enabled; a decrease of 3.51 times. We conclude that implementing on-chain backface culling greatly increases the capacity of Shackled to render complex objects, without any visible change to the output renders.

6   Conclusion and Future Work

In this work, we have introduced and implemented Shackled, the first fully on-chain 3D rendering engine. We have benchmarked its efficiency using three custom datasets, demonstrated its use cases with respect to decentralised rendering, tokenised art, and as a blockchain-based platform for native 3D graphics processing. The datasets, source code, and a user interface for Shackled have been made available publically (see Appendix B). Moreover, we have outlined the challenges associated with implementing complex algorithms (e.g. linear algebraic equations, trigonometry, and tensor operations) entirely in Solidity smart contracts.

In this early stage, Shackled illustrates only a fragment of the potential for fully on-chain algorithms — particularly rendering engines. Candidates for **future work** that could improve Shackled include:

- Removing rendering artifacts along straight lines and edges by implementing the digital differential analyzer algorithm in lieu of Bresenhams algorithm [Koo87], as it is a better fit for interpolating with only integer arithmetic.
- Implementing on-chain rotation transformations using quaternions, Rodrigues' rotation, matrix products, or some other suitable 3D rotation algorithm.
- Taking proper advantage of the 'embarassingly parallel' nature of 3D graphics rendering, e.g. rendering patches of a render simultaneously across nodes and compositing them together once complete.

Acknowledgements. We would like to thank the *entire team at Spectra* for working behind the scenes, sharing ideas which greatly improved the final Shackled renders, and for supporting the development of Shackled and its related projects.

Moreover, running Shackled uses a relatively large gas-equivalent of computation (compared to traditional Ethereum smart contract functions). We would like to thank our partners at *Alchemy* for specially raising the computation limits of an Ethereum read-call on their nodes so as to allow Shackled to operate.

Finally, the creation of Shackled would not have been possible without the *Spectra community*, and we would like to give a warm thanks to Doubtingtrev, HollywoodMeta.eth, Awesomerrificus, and Max Bridgland for their work in directly managing, promoting, supporting, and moderating the community.

In addition, we would like to thank Aubjectivity, nodallydude, Bon(g/j)e, Paul Balaji, Ntando Mhlungu, Divirzion.eth, a7111a.eth, I2DT, wakeupremember.eth, Ian Orz, Animechanic, TriPoloski, ZiK_WaN, NFTxDeFi, Michael Slonim, cearwylm, Petter Rasmussen, rpl.eth, Dalst, reechard.eth, JP, El Citadel, Ralph Clayton, Parker Thompson, Ott Erlord, and Jordysure for their support, feedback, and endorsements of Shackled. Fostering a positive community of folks that are excited about the technological advancement of on-chain art would not have been possible without you all.

Appendix

A   Environmental Considerations

Shackled was developed during the Ethereum blockchain's proof-of-work era. The deployment and subsequent use of the two main contract libraries discussed in this work (Shackled Genesis and Shackled Icons) resulted in a total energy use equivalent to the emission of 54.6 metric tonnes of carbon dioxide, as measured by the Ethereum emissions calculator *Carbon.FYI* [Lim21].

We are aware of the environmental impact of proof-of-work blockchains and have offset five times this amount of carbon dioxide — 273 tonnes — via the retirement of verified carbon credit units provided by *Offsetra Limited.* Verra-accredited retired unit records are available at the following links:

1. https://registry.verra.org/myModule/rpt/myrpt.asp?r=206&h=162735.
2. https://registry.verra.org/myModule/rpt/myrpt.asp?r=206&h=166285.

B   Data Availability and Reproducibility

Data, tools, and code are available at the following links:

- Shackled website.
- Shackled no-code user interface website.
- GitHub repository for accessing datasets.
- Verified smart contracts for Shackled on Etherscan.

References

[Alc22] Alchemy. Alchemy node provider documentation (2022). https://docs. alchemy.com/docs/. Accessed 9 Aug 2022

[B+] Buterin, V., et al.: Ethereum white paper

[Bla19] Blain, J.M.: The Complete Guide to Blender Graphics: Computer Modeling & Animation. AK Peters/CRC Press, Boca Raton (2019)

[Bli77] Blinn, J.F.: Models of light reflection for computer synthesized pictures. In: Proceedings of the 4th Annual Conference on Computer Graphics and Interactive Techniques, pp. 192–198 (1977)

[Bli93] Blinn, J.F.: Backface culling snags (rendering algorithm). IEEE Comput. Graph. Appl. **13**(6), 94–97 (1993)

[Cho21] Chohan, U.W.: Non-fungible tokens: blockchains, scarcity, and value. Crit. Blockchain Res. Initiative (CBRI) Working Papers (2021)

[CPP21] De Collibus, F.M., Partida, A., Piškorec, M.: The role of smart contracts in the transaction networks of four key DeFi-collateral ethereum-based tokens. In: Benito, R.M., Cherifi, C., Cherifi, H., Moro, E., Rocha, L.M., Sales-Pardo, M. (eds.) Conference on Complex Networks and Their Applications X. COMPLEX NETWORKS 2021. Studies in Computational Intelligence, vol. 1015, pp. 792–804. Springer, Cham (2021). https://doi. org/10.1007/978-3-030-93409-5_65

[Dan17] Dannen, C.: Introducing Ethereum and solidity, vol. 1. Springer, Cham (2017)

[fiv21] fiveoutofnine. On chain chess project (2021). https://www.fiveoutofnine. com/

[Fry21] Frye, B.L.: NFTS & the death of art. Available at SSRN 3829399 (2021)

[Gol21] Goldman, M.: Non-fungible tokens: copyright implications in the wild west of blockchain technology (2021)

[GTGB84] Goral, C.M., Torrance, K.E., Greenberg, D.P., Battaile, B.: Modeling the interaction of light between diffuse surfaces. ACM SIGGRAPH Comput. Graph. **18**(3), 213–222 (1984)

[HA21] Harri and Arran. Brotchain. Divergence (2021). https://brotchain.art/

[HMvdW+20] Harris, C.R., et al.: Array programming with NumPy. Nature **585**(7825), 357–362 (2020). https://doi.org/10.1038/s41586-020-2649-2

[Hol22] PROOF Holdings. Moonbirds, the official proof PFP (2022). https:// www.moonbirds.xyz/

[Hub21] Huber, D.: Strange attractors technical details. Strange Attractors (2021). https://strangeattractors.art/details

[Koo87] Koopman, P.: Bresenham line-drawing algorithm. Forth. Dimensions **8**(6), 12–16 (1987)

[Kug21] Kugler, L.: Non-fungible tokens and the future of art. Commun. ACM **64**(9), 19–20 (2021)

[LC79] Lane, J., Carpenter, L.: A generalized scan line algorithm for the computer display of parametrically defined surfaces. Comput. Graph. Image Process. **11**(3), 290–297 (1979)

[Lim21] Offsetra Limited. Carbon fyi (2021). https://carbon.fyi/

[LPC+00] Levoy, M., et al., The digital michelangelo project: 3D scanning of large statues. In: Proceedings of the 27th Annual Conference on Computer Graphics and Interactive Techniques, pp. 131–144 (2000)

[MB08] McHenry, K., Bajcsy, P.: An overview of 3D data content, file formats and viewers. Nat. Cent. Supercomput. Appl. **1205**, 22 (2008)

[MB21] Mackenzie, S., Bērziņa, D.: NFTs: digital things and their criminal lives. Crime, Media, Culture, 17416590211039797 (2021)

[MJ17] Matt and John. Cryptopunks project. Larva Labs (2017). https://www.larvalabs.com/cryptopunks

[MJ19] Matt and John. Autoglyphs project. Larva Labs (2019). https://www.larvalabs.com/autoglyphs

[Nou21] Nouns. Nouns DAO project (2021). https://nouns.wtf/

[Pho75] Bui Tuong Phong: Illumination for computer generated pictures. Commun. ACM **18**(6), 311–317 (1975)

[SA99] Segal, M., Akeley, K.: The OpenGL graphics system: a specification (version 1.1) (1999)

[say22] sayangel. Building the first on-chain 3D NFT with glTF. Blitblox (2022). https://mirror.xyz/angelsay.eth/Fpqj6Hawn-IWGgXm9oEYXyscIgolotYscShuNaVTmI4

[Sta14] Stanford. The stanford 3D scanning repository (2014). https://graphics.stanford.edu/data/3Dscanrep/

[TBDI22] Truby, J., Brown, R.D., Dahdal, A., Ibrahim, I.: Blockchain, climate damage, and death: Policy interventions to reduce the carbon emissions, mortality, and net-zero implications of non-fungible tokens and bitcoin. Energy Res. Soc. Sci. **88**, 102499 (2022)

[TM20] Twomey, D., Mann, A.: Fraud and manipulation within cryptocurrency markets. Corruption Fraud Finan. Markets: Malpract. Misconduct Manipulation, 624 (2020)

[Tok17] Render Token. Render token (RNDR) whitepaper (2017). Accessed 9 Aug 2022

[WB82] Hans Georg Wiedemann and Gerhard Bayer: The bust of Nefertiti. Anal. Chem. **54**(4), 619–628 (1982)

[WJL+20] Ward, I.R., Joyner, J., Lickfold, C., Rowe, S., Guo, Y., Bennamoun, M.: A practical guide to graph neural networks. arXiv preprint arXiv:2010.05234 (2020)

[WLWC21] Wang, Q., Li, R., Wang, Q., Chen, S.: Non-fungible token (NFT): overview, evaluation, opportunities and challenges. arXiv preprint arXiv:2105.07447 (2021)

[Wu21] Wattsy and untokyo. We permanently preserve digital art online. Kohi Art (2021). https://kohi.art/onchain

[Yod22] Yoder, M.: An"OpenSea" of infringement: the intellectual property implications of NFTS. Univ. Cincinnati Intellect. Property Comput. Law J. **6**(2), 4 (2022)

[ZXD+20] An overview on smart contracts: challenges, advances and platforms. Future Gener. Comput. Syst. **105**, 475–491 (2020)

Author Index

Printed in the United States
by Baker & Taylor Publisher Services

Printed in the United States
by Baker & Taylor Publisher Services